NOT FREE AMERICA

NOT FREE AMERICA

WHAT YOUR GOVERNMENT DOESN'T WANT YOU TO KNOW

MIKE DONOVAN

Forefront
BOOKS

*To each and every person who has ever felt the sting of a government
bureaucracy that refuses to hear you and continues to violate your rights.*

To my sons, Sam and Zach.

*To our incredible clients, who have their rights violated every day. You
are the reason I continue to fight for freedom for all.*

*Lastly, to our nation's youth, who are being asked to inherit a nation and economy
that is a shell of what it once was. May the principles in this book help guide our next
generation of leaders, as they fight to make our Not Free America free once more.*

CONTENTS

A NOTE TO THE READER

THIS BOOK DOESN'T "FIT" WELL, MEANING THIS BOOK IS DIFFERENT IN many ways. I hold deep-seated beliefs in the redeeming power of a commitment to individual liberty, and I felt like I needed to write this book in an attempt to save our amazing Republic from crumbling from within.

If you consider yourself left of center, you're really going to love and hate some of the pages in this book. Similarly, if you consider yourself right of center, you may love and hate some of it as well.

Every belief I have is driven by my absolute faith in the rights that were endowed to us by our Creator and enshrined in the Bill of Rights and the Fourteenth Amendment to our Constitution.

I don't ask or expect you to agree with everything I say, but I do appreciate you reading this with an open mind. One thing is for sure, politics—as usual—has brought us to the brink of disaster. We *can* do better, and we must. Doing better means listening to one another and working to fix our ever-compounding liberty crisis in America.

Even though we are living in dark and tumultuous times, I'm profoundly optimistic that if we unite around the concept of liberty, we can create lasting greatness out of our darkest day. The most significant change usually comes from crisis.

If we can just learn to listen to one another, we can really make a difference and ultimately save the American promise of liberty and justice for all.

—MIKE DONOVAN, August 2020

INTRODUCTION

UNDER WHAT AUTHORITY?

THE AMERICA WE ARE LIVING IN RIGHT NOW IS NOT A FREE AMERICA. Once you allow your basic civil liberties to be abridged, it will never stop. When you give away something as precious as your liberty, it's a lot like losing your virginity. You've given away something you'll never get back.

For most people, stability is deeply craved; however, it is instability that spurs the greatest growth. It is part of the human paradox: we sometimes need to go through difficult things to effect positive change. It is interesting now to think back to December 2019. How woefully ignorant and unprepared we all were for the challenges 2020 would present. The walls began closing in on all of us while we were in the throes of the usual year-end activities, celebrating the holidays and looking forward to 2020. Reports began to emerge of a mysterious flu, with pneumonia-like symptoms, linked to an outdoor food market in Wuhan, China. By early January, doctors and researchers were able to determine the illness was a viral pneumonia caused by a new type of coronavirus. At the time, fifty-nine people had been infected, or at least that is what the local authorities were reporting. By the end of the month, the entire Hubei Province was in lockdown.

Maybe you realized something was happening at the time, but, for most Americans, the threat of a global pandemic wasn't even remotely on their radar. We certainly weren't wondering what a response to such a crisis might look like, and we weren't thinking of the risk to American civil liberties that such a response might contain. But we should have been. The first known cases of the new coronavirus confirmed in the US were upon us. Five Americans who had all traveled to Wuhan were infected. Countless others likely were.

The United States government became aware of the coronavirus and its rapid spread in Wuhan in early January—maybe even sooner. But at the time, they reacted as government usually does: They covered up the threat and hoped it would simply go away. They called it a hoax, claimed it wasn't a threat, and assured the citizens of the United States this would simply disappear. The daily denials and playing down of the imminent crisis sent a confusing message. The only organization ringing the alarm was the CDC. And even then, there was conflicting information coming at us like rapid fire.

I call the Commonwealth of Virginia home. By late January, Maryland, Virginia, and the D.C. area were already testing a small number of residents presenting symptoms of the virus. The first two tests they conducted came back negative. For the next few weeks, the health departments around those same areas continued to test. There were no known cases or positive results, alleviating some concern that coronavirus had made its way to our homeland.

Even so, by the last days of January, the World Health Organization (WHO) declared the novel coronavirus a global emergency. Why? The number of cases worldwide had spiked tenfold in a week. By the time the virus ravaged Italy, it was too late. A switch had to be flipped to send a more urgent message about what we would come to know as COVID-19 to persuade people to do the "right thing."

In retrospect, we got it all wrong and, in the process, certain forces among our elite began to attack the sacrosanct rights guaranteed by the American Constitution to all her citizens. Instead of mobilizing efforts to test, treat, and hopefully cure the virus, the vast majority of American governmental resources at both the state and federal level were appropriated to convince us to hide, be controlled, and depend on our governors and president for our very lives so we did not notice their lack of preparedness and inability to manage a global health crisis.

By the end of February, the United States recorded its first coronavirus death—a man in his fifties at a long-term health care facility in Washington State. Soon after, the news of other positive cases and deaths were beginning to pop up around the country.

In Virginia, a US Marine stationed at Fort Belvoir tested positive on March 10. By this time, the country was spiraling out of control. Coast to coast, people were panicking, rushing to their local grocery stores, and stocking up on essential items, as if a Category 5 hurricane were coming. Retail stores were closing, some boarded up, and large gatherings were being cancelled or postponed.

Whether you realize it or not, while the government was suddenly scrambling to find enough ventilators and PPE supplies, they were also making a conscious decision to restrict your liberty. They didn't trust you enough not to take appropriate measures to safely go to church, so they shut the churches down. They didn't trust you enough to take precautions to safely go to the mall, the beach, or the park, so they shut those down too.

The day before Virginia officially locked down on March 30, I unexpectedly found myself in the mall in Charlottesville with my father. The Charlottesville mall is a large regional shopping center that's usually packed with people. When we pulled in, there were only a few cars in the parking lot.

Although the governor had not yet announced the shelter in place order, we all knew it was coming. The writing was on the wall. As we searched for a Starbucks, we couldn't help but notice there were only three stores open that day. A sign in the storefront of Aéropostale read, We love you. We miss you. Stay safe, stay healthy, wear a mask. Each of the store's sales associates had signed it. The few people wandering the mall were writing hopeful notes on the various signs. One read, "It's never going to be the same again."

I paused and thought about that as I stood there in a deserted mall with my father. Growing up he was my rock and anchor. As an adult, he has come to work for me and my companies. And yet, in that moment, I became a child again, and I thanked God that my anchor was still there.

It was surreal.

Was this our new normal?

In the days leading up to this, I'd watched larger cities such as New York, Los Angeles, Detroit, and Chicago shutter. The videos that emerged of the empty streets, not a soul to be seen, were breathtaking. One by one, cities and small towns closed while people stayed locked up in their own homes. That vast, empty landscape could only be described as something I had once seen in *The Walking Dead,* except there were no zombies—only scared Americans trying to figure out what to do next.

An hour earlier, I had taken my son Zach to the hospital because he was having severe anxiety around the pandemic. Zach had suffered prior childhood trauma before he came to live with us, and negative world events affect him more than most children. With the nonstop coverage on the news, he literally thought the world was ending. And to some degree, that was what the media outlets were saying. The news was overwhelming and, for some, downright unbearable. After six full days of no sleep, an accidental breaking of his bedroom window, and an increasing level of paranoia that was difficult to control, we could no longer care for Zach at home. Though we were fearful of his potential exposure to the coronavirus in this strange new world, ultimately, we needed to make the choice to get him emergency medical help.

By the time we arrived at the hospital, it was a struggle just to get Zach into a wheelchair. When someone you love is suffering from panic and fear, there is very little you can do or say to alleviate those feelings. I just needed to reassure him that I loved him and that everything was going to be alright. There was no mistaking the sense of dread Richard, my partner, and I had that day. The emergency room was full of sick people, some, perhaps, with COVID-19. Some were masked; others weren't. And the staff seemed to be too overwhelmed to enforce their own policy that masks were necessary. I tried to convince my son to put on a mask, that it was for his own good. He said he couldn't breathe, and I felt helpless. I had no idea who was in that emergency room. Were they infected? Were we? When would I see my child again?

I noticed a woman standing about ten feet away from us, crying. A nurse who had been barking orders at me suddenly turned to her and said, "Okay. You have to come in now."

"No, I want to leave," the woman said.

"You can't leave. You have COVID-19 symptoms. We need to test you." The nurse was firm and obviously annoyed.

"Can I leave after?" the woman asked.

"If you test positive, you can't leave until the doctor says you can."

I turned to the nurse and asked, "Under what authority can you tell this woman that she's held here?"

One thing you should know about me is that I often get in the middle of other people's conversations, especially when it comes to preserving our civil liberties and rights as Americans. As a civil and human rights activist, I knew the nurse didn't have the authority she was exercising. So again, I asked, "By what authority do you have the right to keep this woman against her will?"

The nurse turned to me and snapped, "By the authority vested in the public health and welfare by the government." And just like that, she turned around and walked away.

I struggled for a moment to remember where exactly this power was granted to the government in the United States Constitution. Of course, it doesn't exist.

Within minutes, the hospital had a security guard come and grab the woman by the arm and take her into triage.

"Where are we?" I thought. "This is not the United States of America."

A minute or two later, the same nurse returned and said, "I'm having *you* arrested if you don't get off of hospital property."

"For what?" I asked. "My son is here, and I am not leaving him."

"I don't care. You're not staying," she said.

With the snap of her fingers, the same security guard who took the woman away was coming for me. Shockingly, I was forced, against my will and rights, to abandon my child in the middle of a crisis. The hospital had let my partner go back with Zach to register him, and in the interest of getting him the best care, I decided to leave. If Richard hadn't been there, I would not have left. I'm not sure what I would have done, and the gravity of that thought still weighs on me today. I also wonder every day whether I will have to make this decision for any of my loved ones who may enter a hospital during a public health crisis in the future.

As we all now know, the coronavirus pandemic was *not* a hoax. It is and was very real and, at the time, was spreading through our country like wildfire. The information being shared was conflicting and changing daily. I don't believe the coronavirus was a ruse, either. I believe it was one of the single biggest human health crises we've seen in our country. However, the true danger of coronavirus was never that it would be an event that caused human extinction. The true danger of coronavirus, and our reaction to it, is that it may very well lead to the extinction of individual liberty.

Ironically, it seemed the novel coronavirus attacked American civil liberties as furiously as it attacked the bodies of those infected. In times like these, the true value of being a *free* citizen is realized. COVID-19 is a very serious disease, one that became like the perfect storm to allow our government to grab the constitutional rights of Americans.

The tension between private liberty and public health in America is hardly new. Dating back to the Colonial era, Americans have demanded health and safety from its government during times of plague and pandemics while expecting liberty at all other times. The manipulation of the people by politicians and heads of business has equally been used and abused for nearly as long.

Quarantines in America date back as early as 1701. Members of the Massachusetts Bay Colony spent a year fighting against protesters who wanted to stand in the way of the first quarantine orders, saying they were too harsh. There were people who felt exactly the same way during the Spanish flu pandemic of 1918 and, of course, in 2020 during the COVID-19 pandemic. Short-term limits on some liberties are fine when those limitations are effectuated through education or even propaganda, but American ideals demand that the choice ultimately must rest with the individual.

Most rational thinking people support temporary measures to slow the spread of a virus. But the virus arrived while we were at a fundamental fork in the road and became a symptom of a much bigger problem in the country—the suspension of the Constitution during a time of great crisis. Instead of having serious conversations with the American people about the impending crisis, the government passed unusual restrictions on travel, assembly, worship, working, and general living. That's also what allowed our government to pause court proceedings, detain people indefinitely without trials, and enforce stay at home orders, just to name a few of the un-American realities associated with a post-COVID-19 society. While your civil liberties might feel less important when thousands of people are dying of a disease with no known treatment or cure, they should be a primary concern. Those responses can and often do easily tip into misuse and abuse or can become part of our daily lives after the threat has passed. We saw this after the attacks on 9/11 when our government created the Patriot Act.

As we look at the COVID-19 death toll, do we really want to add the death of democracy in the United States of America to the list?

Think back for a moment about the way things were in our country before COVID-19. Would you have ever given any credence to the police using force to prevent you from peacefully protesting, going to work, or leaving your home? How about telling you that enjoying a walk in the park, eating out, shopping, worshiping, or gathering for any reason was no longer your choice? When did the government go from being *of* the people, *by* the people, and *for* the people to presiding *over* its people?

When I was a little boy, my grandmother told me that in good times, everybody is your friend and everything is great. It's only when bad times come around that you begin to understand who your friends really are, who is going to be there for you, and what it means to be alone in a crisis. This is one of many incredibly important life lessons I received from my grandmother, a Cherokee Native American who cared for her family like an eagle. Many people who live in the United States of America have not felt that, and certainly not at a level where they would question whether their government would be able to meet their needs.

I have news for you. The government was not able to meet our needs. During the pandemic, our government didn't have the resources stockpiled to provide hospitals with enough respirators to keep Americans alive. It didn't have protective gear to distribute to the frontline workers. And it didn't properly prepare for your health and welfare. Americans died unnecessarily because we didn't have the equipment to keep them alive and, worse, because there was a bigger agenda being served. Hopefully, we will be able to learn important lessons from these unconscionable inactions and what happens when the darkest times of humanity meet the most desperate—but I wouldn't count on it.

As an American citizen and having been a resident, at various times, of Virginia, California, Minnesota, and Colorado, I've never known my governor to tell me I couldn't leave my house. I've never known my governor to tell me I couldn't go to a movie or meet up with a group of friends. I've never known my governor to tell me that my church must close because we aren't allowed to assemble.

Accepting this was hard. While I knew these same orders existed in the majority of the United States, my governor, Ralph Northam of Virginia, executed two executive orders under the Commonwealth of Virginia Emergency Services and Disaster Law of 2000. In that statute, the governor is empowered to "proclaim and publish such rules and regulations and to issue such orders as may, in his judgment, be necessary to accomplish the purposes of this chapter . . ." The purpose of the disaster statute is to confer upon the governor emergency powers "in order to insure that preparations of the Commonwealth and its political subdivisions will be adequate to protect the public peace, health, and safety, and to preserve the lives and property and economic well-being of the people of the Commonwealth."[1] Simply stated, the legislature conferred upon the governor in that statute unlimited and unbridled power. His only restriction is his judgment.

When we elect officials, we do so because we trust their judgment. We authorize them to protect our rights and prevent them from interfering with our personal liberties. That trust, however, isn't blind. We have a series of checks and balances in place, and the legislature cannot abandon its responsibilities to the people, limiting the governor's executive authority only by his "judgment."

This revelation was extraordinary to me. We were giving away too much power. It didn't matter if the governor or the president weren't abusing the power. Once we give that power away, we likely never get it back.

We're Americans. We fight wars, disease, and tyranny. We are a nation born out of a revolution—a war we fought to get out from under the monarchy of England. Our founding fathers created the very basis of this country by establishing a government dedicated to the liberty of its people over the false impression of safety. Freedom was so important to the founders that they embedded their choice in the Declaration of Independence, which states that no government is legitimate without the consent of the governed and that government's principal duty is to secure our rights and the United States Constitution, which expressly protects the right to make personal choices. *That* is the supreme law of the land, and therefore all government acts are subordinate to it.

Our government has failed its first obligation—to safeguard our freedoms. Their negligence and disregard for the needs of its people has shifted how we as a country operate. The very thing that unites us through our struggles is that we are a free people, and it is us, the people of the United States, who get to choose what's best for us—not our government.

Blindly accepting the restrictions the government places on us, even during times of crisis, is a test, not so much in what we will do in response to this crisis but rather what will we give away in the process.

When the governor shut down the Charlottesville mall on March 30, 2020, he took away any chance those stores had to make money to pay their leases, keep their employees earning, and keep the economy in Virginia going. On what constitutional authority did he and the other governors and mayors do this? While the right of success is not a guaranteed right, equal access and opportunity are absolute rights in this country. Macy's or Bath & Body Works might survive such an order, but the likelihood of a small mom-and-pop shop getting through such uncharted waters was very low. In the United States, small businesses are responsible for 39 percent of the gross national product. Additionally, 52 percent of all US sales contribute about 21 percent of all manufactured US exports. Small businesses contribute 44 percent of all sales in the country. And now, the local, mom-and-pop store didn't have a national platform on which to justify itself. All the jobs were gone. It's as close to a post-apocalyptic event as this country has ever seen. And we're not accustomed to that.

And as if that isn't bad enough, we haven't seen anything yet.

America's struggles may have just begun, and our darkest days may lie ahead.

I am the president and CEO of Nexus Services and the pastor of First Christian Church Universalist of Harrisonburg. Our church was founded in 2014 as a parish and a social-justice ministry. Our work there has focused its ministry on people re-entering society from jail and prison. The church's efforts have assisted in the successful release of thousands of people from incarceration, leading them to full societal participation.

By the time the stay-at-home orders were put into place, I knew my parishioners needed church more than ever. To me, spiritual health is as important as physical health, especially in trying times. Yet the governor was telling us we couldn't meet. It didn't make sense to me, especially if the members of my congregation were willing to abide by the social-distancing recommendations and wear masks. We'd seen churches do this with disastrous consequences, but we also saw churches reopen while respecting social distancing and CDC recommendations without consequence. There's nothing more American than free people making their own choices about how we live our lives. The orders we all adhered to across this great nation were mostly all patently unconstitutional. And as someone who greatly believes in the unalienable rights guaranteed in the Constitution, I wasn't willing to stand down.

My father raised me to believe that when something is uncomfortable, you have to choose to go through it so you can get it out of the way, and you have to go through it with the most energy, vigor, and aggression because that's how you will get through it faster. I grew up with that philosophy drilled into my head, so this imbalance of power, this stripping down of liberty, felt so incredibly wrong.

While I could intellectualize that the virus was dangerous and it would infect and, yes, kill people, the aftermath was destined to be far worse than if we had just faced it with the resources of the federal government to get proper testing in place and to find the treatment we needed. Maybe more people would have died initially if we had taken that approach, and that would have been horrible, but it would have killed far fewer people than will die in the next five years because of poverty. This may not be a popular sentiment, but I believe it's true. Sometimes the truth isn't what we want to hear, but we must listen.

I could no longer pretend that we were going to beat this great enemy by dissolving the civil liberties of Americans. Such a prescription gives us a cure more debilitating than the virus. America achieves because its people reach for the stars. In times of adversity, we are known for getting serious and fixing problems. Our faith communities spring into action, feeding the poor and tending to the needs of our communities. And yet, now, those same faith-based communities were ordered shuttered by the government.

Our government told us to trust them, to accept the wholesale shredding of the Bill of Rights. It used to be a given that the government we elected would work for the people it serves. Today, that power has shifted. We founded this country to get out from under the rule of a tyrant trying to tell its people how to live. Here we are, 243 years later, facing the very same decision.

If we allow our government to divorce its people from the process and send them to hide under their beds, the result will be fascism and tyranny, the likes of which this nation hasn't seen in hundreds of years.

I

WE ARE NOT FREE

What will become of America?
What will become of us?
What kind of country will our children inherit?

THINK ABOUT SOMETHING YOU'RE REALLY AFRAID OF. SOMETHING THAT keeps you awake at night. Maybe it's a death in the family or the loss of your job.

Think about that uneasy feeling you get when you imagine the worst-case scenario of losing something precious—the fear you have when realizing you don't know what to do.

What I am describing is where we are right now as a country.

Whether we realize it or not, all of us in the United States of America are living with some type of governmental restriction on our constitutionally protected liberties. Instead of providing resources to help citizens thrive, our lawmakers are passing legislation that threatens jail if we exercise certain constitutional and basic human rights. We are desperately trying to get off a roller coaster that has already left the platform and is making its way up the steep hill. If you've ever been to an amusement park, you know the feeling: It's too late to get off this ride.

At one point during the pandemic, about 90 percent of Americans were under shut-down orders and most states banned gatherings of any kind. And just as we were emerging from those restraints, mandatory curfews were implemented in cities across the country due to nonpeaceful protesting and civil unrest brought about from the murder of George Floyd by four Minneapolis police officers.

Should this have been a surprise?

Not at all.

Humans are defined not by the crises they endure, but by how they respond and overcome. When individuals exercising liberty respond to crisis, we win. When the response is the American police state, we all lose.

For the past ten years, I have been closely monitoring the bubbling up of these long-held, pent-up emotions, slowly witnessing, along with you and everyone else, what seems like the very thread of our society unraveling. To many of us, it seems as if we are witnessing the fall of American democracy as we know it.

My company, Nexus Services, funds thousands of civil rights lawsuits. I've walked with people through some of the worst and most unimaginable abuses: police abuse, abuse by our court system, and abuse by our tax codes, as well as the wholesale slaughter of Americans, black and white, at the hands of their unaccountable police.

The last time the world experienced a global health crisis like the COVID-19 pandemic was in 1918. There was no internet, no social media, and none of the connectivity we have today. It was a much smaller world, but one that was much more dangerous for individuals, as individuals were responsible for their day-to-day lives. It has been a few generations since Americans had to do any heavy lifting to save the promise our founders enshrined in our Constitution. Our generation, and that of our children, will be the next American generation who determine whether this amazing experiment in representative democracy continues to thrive or whether it dies.

And if you aren't certain yet that we are dying, consider this:

When the people of the United States of America are being arrested for attending weddings, funerals, and places of worship, America is dying.

When there is a basic shortage of essential items such as food and medicine, America is dying.

When people are unemployed and unable to work, America is dying.

When there is a politicization on basic hygiene, American is dying.

When the people of the United States are being shot by their police officers who are protected by their unions and the apathy of the people of the country, America may already be dead.

With those things happening, *of course* there is going to be an uprising unlike anything we've ever seen in our lifetime. It's a simple matter of numbers. When we get to a boiling point where our acceptance of persecution and oppression outweighs our yearning for liberty, the system will collapse—or worse, the government will take full control, which is really the same thing. Either way, representative democracy will be at serious risk.

Are we ready for the system to collapse around us?

Are we willing to submit to the government to decide whether we can leave our homes, whether we can go to our family celebrations, or whether and when we can seek medical attention?

Does the social order we deserve really require draconian, big-government solutions that take away our civil liberties?

The United States of America is better than this. The American people are better than this. We are a nation that eradicated smallpox. We are a nation that saved the world from fascism, communism, and totalitarianism. We are not a nation that hides under our beds in a crisis. We are a nation of people who get to work and *resolve* crises.

We've never seen a clearer picture than we have in the year 2020 that when things are secure, everything is great, but when that security breaks, everything we depend on stops working. And unless we define and defend what it is that makes us free—unless we unite to defend it—we will lose it all.

Here's what I mean.

Our government is spending money it doesn't have. Our states are bankrupt or going broke. Our municipalities are crushed under debt overburdened by the pandemic and the aftermath. It will take generations to rebuild any sense of security in this country—financial, physical, and emotional security. It will take months and perhaps even years to even calculate the true economic impact of our national shutdown. And as the unprecedented trillions in stimulus monies dry up, the false positives of that money will leave our economy and it will take generations to rebuild what has been destroyed. And that rebuilding will only work if the good people of this country on the right and left can come together. Given our divisions, will we be able to unite today for our civil rights so that we may continue to have the right to disagree tomorrow?

That's up to us.

We may well be in the throes of a new civil war, but most Americans don't even realize they're in battle. While we sit home watching the country burn, we are simultaneously witnessing our basic and most fundamental rights being violated. Yet we tolerate it. Worse, we accept it. We may be losing our last opportunity to divert our country from a path that leads only to destruction from within to a path that recognizes the sacramental nature of our liberty. We may just lose the opportunity to stop this war from spreading to all of our cities and towns, not just our largest. We need to trust the power and resolve of the free American people to overcome this and any challenge to our security. We overcome insecurity with strength and passion, not by cowering in fear.

Viktor Frankl was an Austrian neurologist and psychiatrist, as well as a Holocaust survivor. Prior to being captured by the Nazis and taken to four different concentration camps, including Auschwitz, he had begun writing a composition about human motivation that challenged Abraham Maslow's hierarchy of needs. Maslow had indicated that unless your basic needs are met, you cannot do things that are transcendent. In Frankl's 1946 book *Man's Search for Meaning*, he expressed the view—further confirmed by his Holocaust experiences—that finding meaning in one's life, no matter how dire the suffering one endures, is what leads to transcendence.

His office in Vienna, where he lived after the war, was filled with twenty-nine honorary degrees, including his medical degree, his PhD in philosophy, and, oddly, a ratty certificate for solo-piloting a Cessna in San Diego when he was in his late sixties. When asked about the flying certificate one day, he explained that he really enjoyed hiking and mountain climbing. Despite his love of adventure, he had developed an aversion to flying over the years. It wasn't until he was in his sixties that he decided he and his wife should learn to pilot an aircraft. His reason was simple: "There are some things about myself I don't have to tolerate."

You see, tolerance has its limits. And it is hard to tolerate what is itself intolerable. This America is intolerable. It isn't who we are, and the truth is, we simply don't have to accept it. Martin Luther King once said, "Our lives begin to end when we become silent about the things that matter." The perception of freedom is that what we accept becomes the acceptable. There are consequences for every choice. Some consequences should not be tolerated, and some consequences lead us to places a free America was never meant to go, places where a free America can't survive.

When I went to law school, one of my professors taught us that a good lawyer has to learn not to care. Law students are taught not to get personally vested in a case. We were told that if we cared too much, we would lose our objectivity. I thought his advice was an oxymoronic concept. How could I do that—not care? Sure, if I don't care about playing tennis, then I don't play tennis. I know I will never play tennis because to me, I don't care about it. I don't find it interesting.

But I don't understand people who can "not care" about fellow humans. I don't understand how people can see an issue yet walk away from it, hoping someone else will fix it. Isn't there a level of responsibility that comes with knowing something? Not just thinking it, but truly knowing it to be real? My parents taught me this. School taught me this. Jesus of Nazareth teaches me this every day in my study of His teachings and my spiritual relationship with Him. Every major world religion, in fact, teaches responsibility over the things you know. In fact, it is simply natural law. When you ignore responsibility, you seal a fate of suffering the weight of your hypocrisy. And *that* is precisely where America is today. On COVID-19, on police relations, on race, on economic disparity, and on any number of other issues that could literally rip civil society apart. Are you ready to take responsibility yet?

If you choose inaction, you become part of the problem.

Once you know something, it's awfully hard to unknow it. Sure, you can ignore it, pretend it's not real or your problem, but that doesn't mean it isn't happening. Look at apartheid, Nazi Germany, genocide in Darfur, America's historic mistreatment of minorities and women, the HIV/AIDS crisis, and the list goes on and on. If you choose to look the other way when it comes to your constitutional rights, that is the same as tolerating that decision and therefore accepting the consequences. You can't complain when you're unable to get back what you've chosen so freely to give up.

I'm a business owner who employs hundreds of people through various entities. Nexus Services focuses our efforts on serving people in crisis. In 2014, I founded Libre by Nexus to serve those who are victims of a broken immigration and criminal-justice system. Our company is an alternative to immigration detention for undocumented immigrants who cannot pay collateral for bonds. My vision was to liberate immigrants who have been subject to the defects of the current system. I began Libre by Nexus to help people who are incarcerated after personally experiencing unfair bond process and the financial burden unreasonably high bonds inflict. From the inception, Libre by Nexus has worked to ensure that our program is centered on the principle of respecting and affirming the inherent worth and dignity of every person. Many of our employees have navigated the flawed immigration system themselves and understand firsthand how tumultuous the immigration process can be. Our company grew quickly, and we have had a level of success that we never anticipated, growing from a single location in Virginia to over twenty offices nationwide. Because of this growth, we can better serve those seeking a new life in the United States.

Empower by Nexus is another division of our company that works with those re-entering society to ensure they are able to make a life for themselves post incarceration. Even our property-management company works specifically to help people who struggle to qualify for traditional rentals find a welcome place to rebuild their lives. From the start, the focus of our company has been on servicing and ministering to those who are suffering by reuniting families who have been negatively impacted by the broken immigration system.

We believe that detaining anyone for extended periods of time without providing access to legal counsel is unacceptable. That's why we fund Nexus Derechos Humanos Attorneys (NDH), a law firm that works to increase access to justice for disadvantaged people across the United States. This is part of what we call our "directed-giving" campaign, where the vast majority of our profits are reinvested in actual service work to better the lives of the people we serve. After all, we are a nation of immigrants.

Some of the lawsuits we file are called "section 1983" suits, referring to a portion of the federal code that allows Americans to sue a state that violates their rights. Other suits we file are called "Bivens claims," which are similar but can be filed against a federal agent or official. In funding this work, I have seen horrors most people can't imagine are happening in this country—from a sheriff who forced inmates to be sterilized to the shooting of a toddler who was in the way of a police officer attempting to execute a family dog.

Both forms of lawsuits are always extremely difficult to try because the government is your adversary in cases like these, and typically the victim is disaffected and disenfranchised. In many cases, the defendants are under probation supervision, which can put their freedom in jeopardy on a whim. People who are victimized and innocent often won't litigate these claims because of a legal doctrine called "qualified immunity," which has become the subject of much political debate in the wake of recent protests and which is the subject of a subsequent chapter in this book. As a ruling in one of our cases, *Pearson v. Callahan*, stated: "Qualified immunity is a type of legal immunity which balances two important interests—the need to hold public officials accountable when they exercise power irresponsibly and the need to shield officials from harassment, distraction, and liability when they perform their duties reasonably."[2]

In reality, qualified immunity protects criminal gangsters wearing government costumes, who are the police in name only and rain tyranny down on fellow Americans without consequence and do all this with the government's support.

This means that cases of horrific abuse rarely make it even to a federal district court, much less an appellate court, because the likelihood of sustaining a claim is very low. Unfortunately, when these cases don't get filed, the appellate courts can't weigh in and these injustices don't matter and therefore can't have an impact on the law. That result is inconsistent with a basic liberty interest and, more importantly, incongruent to the promise of America—namely that we are a free people with the absolute right to due process. When I say "liberty interest," what I am talking about is the very basic promise of America. That promise is that you and I get to make our own choices about our lives. That is not the role of the ruling elites.

The 1983 and Bivens claim cases that we fight for every day represent the front line between an out-of-control police state and the people of these United States. The ability to sue the police has been severely limited over the past fifty years, but these statutes still provide a narrow vehicle to punish injustice. That window closes every day, and unless we adopt a liberty principle as a foundation of our government, the fight will move from these front lines to your homes. If you don't help fight for liberty now, you won't have anyone left to fight with you later. In other words, you may die at the hands of a fascist government because you're not willing to stand up for your individual liberty right now.

We fund these cases for two specific reasons. One, the cases are critical to the issue of police power in this country. If police have a lesser standard and expectation than everyday Americans, how could we ever expect them to lead by example? Why is it so controversial to assert that our police should be the best in the world? Don't we believe we should always attempt to be the best in the world at everything? It's an American ideal. We can't accomplish that idea until we decide what rules we are going to use, and I argue we must unite around a core principle of individual liberty.

The second reason we fund these cases is because my faith teaches me that I am to seek out and serve the meek and the weak. I follow Jesus' example in the way I live my life. When fighting for the God-given rights of the American people, I am able to serve God. This isn't something special, by the way; it is something each and every one of us can and should do in our own way.

I see a radical shift happening that every one of us needs to be aware of—abdicating our civil liberties to allow big government to get even bigger. Let us not forget

the promise of the Declaration of Independence, the American Constitution, the Bill of Rights, and the Fourteenth Amendment, which guarantees due process and the American people's ability to remain free. *That* is what is under assault and what we're fighting for. A significant minority, composed of black, brown, and poor white people, have lived without those rights in a veritable American police state. In light of the coronavirus, we've all seen how easy it is to lose our rights.

If you really think about it, rights are not rights if they aren't guaranteed to all Americans. If they are guaranteed only to some, they are *privileges* and not *rights*. Our Bill of Rights addresses absolute rights; it does not discuss privileges.

A free America can no longer survive on a false promise built on a bed of privilege. When a privilege trumps an absolute right, we are all doomed. Why? Because privileges can always be taken away.

If you're completely comfortable with the idea of privileges being more important than rights, there are plenty of places in the world where the government will tell you exactly what to do every second, every minute, every hour of the day.

But that is not America. At least it didn't used to be.

Do you really think we're free?

Think again.

For a long time, I thought I was free, a certainty that is extremely important to me. Freedom in the United States was never a Democratic or a Republican, a conservative or a liberal belief. No, for me, it has always been my *guarantee* as an American. It is the founding principle on which this country was built. Over the course of many years of struggle, I think it is safe to say we have lost our way. We have drifted so far from the vision our founders had for this country and you know what? You should be scared. Scared for the future, if there is a future, and worried about the impact our complacency will have on your children's lives and their children's too. I know I am scared for my family and my employees, but that fear must motivate us to rise above.

Everyone wants freedom. For some, it may well mean breaking free from a job they hate or a miserable marriage. Afterward, it's not uncommon to regret that decision. Some people feel like they had something solid they should never have let go of. Those people don't want the accountability of freedom because sometimes the outcome can be unpleasant. There's a level of stability with not being free, just as there is instability or certainty that comes with absolute freedom. Do you want to be comfortable or do you choose to run the marathon, forever fighting for your place in history?

Do we only achieve real freedom when we die?

Of course not.

Freedom is contextual. And often, freedom presents as many obstacles as it does opportunities. The difference is obstacles are something we can face ourselves without relying on Grandpa Government to somehow take care of us. When we manage obstacles on our own, we are much more likely to serve our interests. That is a choice.

What our government has learned from its people and our willingness to be herded like sheep is that our rights are not precious enough for us to stand up for, much less fight for them. And when we do, it often serves as the very thing that drives the American government into reform. But, if we don't speak up and demand better from our government, then, rest assured, in the area of civil liberties—yours and mine—normal doesn't exist anymore.

When you think about it, the human plane of existence can be represented by a piece of college-ruled paper. If you look at that piece of paper, you'd see two margins, one on the left and one on the right. Most people live, or at least want to live, in the middle of that page. The middle of that page represents stability because it's the furthest point from any of the corners. Everyone congregates in the middle because it's where they feel the safest and most secure. They're wealthy and they've got all the power, and, as a result, they start building lines and limits to protect what they have. They keep people away from the center of the page by pushing them further and further away from the margins until people eventually just fall off the page. Most people spend their entire lives on a journey to try and get to the center of the page.

The American police state needs the majority of the people to want to live in the middle to keep law and order. If people don't realize what is happening to them, then they are easily controlled. If the government can make sure the vast majority of the people aren't experiencing these rights abuses, then those people will not care that a certain number of people are.

How do you do that?

It's simple.

You don't police white communities like you police black and brown communities. You don't police wealthy communities like you police poor communities.

Why?

Poor people are less stable and live closer to the outer edges of that piece of paper.

The elites ruling this country need a subclass of people. And that subclass is turned through the criminal-justice system, the immigration-justice system, and all of our different government programs every day. Every economy of scale is based on gluttony. And gluttony requires the abdication of things of necessity from certain people. Everything is a balance. Some people will tell you that the biggest danger of gluttony is when a person or corporation hoards wealth. I believe that gluttony is most dangerous when the subject is power and the powerful is your elite government. *That* obsession with power may kill us all.

The biggest crisis this elitist government faces is when that balance no longer works and a number of people decide they're not okay because they've lost faith in the government. That's when things go off the rails. That's America in 2020.

Now, some people actually choose to live in the margins. They don't like the center and don't want to be anywhere near safety or security. Those people tend to be our greatest and worst people in society. They are the true difference makers and history makers. Some use their power for good and others for evil. That power is their willingness to actually live and make a difference. Either way, they will effect change. Jesus definitely chose to live in the margins of the page, living among and serving the freaks, weirdos, and disappointments. The most fundamentally transformative thing is that Jesus did not think of himself as better than those He served. He understood that His perspective, no matter how broad or narrow it might be,

would be different than those He served. He listened. He cared. And He led. And without a piece of property or any real money to His name, He became one of the single most important people in human history. He chose to live in the margins and serve, and He is my teacher.

Most of our founders were men and women who lived in the margins too. A free people with limited government will appreciate these pioneers. An elitist government will resist these people because the government sees them as a threat. That's me—one of the people the government seeks to destroy because they pose a threat. What threat do I pose, you ask? The threat I pose is the worst threat of all to an elitist government—I give people information and hope. Hope can change hearts, and it can inspire people for greatness.

Understand, true freedom is a radical concept. It's one of the most sought-after ideals in human history. The concept in America began with the colonists, who were unwavering men and women in search of religious tolerance that had been denied them under King George. They were seeking a better life rooted in that kind of freedom. During his famous farewell address, George Washington said, "Of all the dispositions and habits which lead to political prosperity, religion and morality are indispensable supports." The foundations of our national policy had to be laid in the pure and immutable principles of private morality.

When the American framers wrote the Constitution, they intended to prevent abuse of power by carefully defining the specific responsibilities and narrowly restricting the administrative powers of all three governmental branches. The highest authority in the land wasn't any particular branch of government or any elected official. It was the United States Constitution. The Supreme Rule of Law. Rule of Law, which some also refer to as "constitutionalism," is the restriction of the arbitrary exercise of power by subordinating it to well-defined and established laws. The Oxford English Dictionary defines it as "authority and influence of law in society and the guiding principle whereby all members of a society (including those in government) are considered equally subject to the law." If exceptions are made, the rule of law begins to collapse. Unfortunately, our elite government makes exceptions every day.

The founders of this nation established our government dedicated to liberty over the illusion of safety. They embedded that choice into the Declaration of

Independence as well as the Constitution. The Declaration of Independence clearly states that no government is legitimate without the consent of the governed and that the government's principal duty is to secure our rights. The Constitution expressly protects the right to make personal choices, and that is the supreme law of the land. All governmental acts are subordinate to it. Shouldn't our government be safeguarding our freedoms? I think so. Except for one thing. That would have to mean we are, in fact, free. And we're not.

The concept of supreme law isn't a new one. It can be found within the pages of the Old Testament. In fact, it can be found peppered through the religions and faith traditions through much of the world. The idea is that God grants us certain rights as a result of creation and the endowment of rights consistent with free will. And along with those rights come responsibilities, and chief among them is the responsibility to protect your rights. If our rights are endowed by God, they can't be taken away by government. If you allow the government to usurp your God-given rights, you are placing the government above God in your life. Do you really want to do that?

Not everyone will exercise their constitutional rights every day. Some people won't exercise them for long periods of time, but that doesn't make them less important. They have to not just be codified, not just recognized, but immortalized. It has to be a part of who we are, to our core. And if you are an "ends justify the means" person, that's a very dangerous thing. If you believe in a liberty interest, then the ends can't possibly justify the means. Why? Because the ends don't really matter. The means do. If the path we travel doesn't matter, then ethics don't matter. That's why we fight every day against corruption in the American police state. Because the means matter most. We know we are in a long fight, and the arc of justice favors the patient when fighting a government or government agency.

Jesus' teachings are right on point. When His adversaries tried to trick Him by asking whether it was appropriate for the Jews, whose nation had been taken over by the Roman Empire, to pay tribute to the Roman emperor, His answer was simple: "Render therefore unto Caesar the things which are Caesar's; and unto God the things that are God's" (Matthew 22:21). If Caesar controls your rights, they're Caesar's rights; they're not yours. But if God gave you those rights, then they're not Caesar's to take away.

These words from the book of Matthew are why our Declaration of Independence reads that we have certain unalienable rights endowed by our creator. "We are endowed by our creator." Why did they use those words? Specifically, because it is a foundational understanding. The idea that everybody has a choice is the ultimate free will, especially when interacting with your government. How many times has this been perverted in the history of this this country and how great is it that we are able to keep having fights and discussions over it? What we are really talking about is that the fight we have in front of us right now is to preserve the ability to fight about other stuff tomorrow. If we don't stand up and fight for the liberty principle now, we won't be able to fight about anything later. Someone else will make decisions for us about everything...and that's not the America I want to live in. I'd rather die than live in that place. I've lived an amazing life where I made choices to build businesses that have reached incredible heights. And we got there by being focused and principled.

In life and in politics, there must be some kind of principle, something that you anchor your boat to. And it has to be strong.

According to our founding fathers, that principle comes from God—our heavenly Father—not from the founding fathers, and so the current government can't take it away. God gave us life; the government did not. The government can't and shouldn't be able to take my life away on a whim. If my right to be free comes from God, then only God can take it away. A system of justice predicated on due process is a godly system because it recognizes individual liberty as a core principle.

Today, America is failing. Those who should be enforcing the Constitution are instead working, actively and openly, to undermine the very law on which our country was established.

Some of us have known America has been heading in the wrong direction for years, and despite this spirit of lawlessness that has permeated the highest degrees of government, we still cannot conceive that we as a nation could end up in anarchy, let alone captivity or slavery.

But that's exactly where we are headed.

And we are seeing signs of it every day.

Together we can save America. Together we can leave our kids a country of which they can be proud. Together we can fight for the civil liberties of all people.

If we don't make some changes, and I mean now, there will be no turning back. What we choose to tolerate becomes acceptable. The intolerable becomes tolerable. And that's no longer an option. At least not to me.

However, I'm strangely optimistic at the same time. I know that every moment of greatness comes with great risk of peril, and every moment of darkness comes with a great opportunity for light. Times may be scary. They may be tough. But we are Americans. We aren't afraid of a fight and we have always been willing to stand up for what we believe in. We always anticipated that threat would come from across the world, but our founders predicted it would come from within. They knew our greatest enemy would be ourselves.

We pulled ourselves back together once, and if we work together, we just might be able to divert America's next civil war.

2

OUR ABUSIVE RELATIONSHIP WITH THE GOVERNMENT

THE CHIEF OF HUMAN RESOURCES AT NEXUS SERVICES IS A CONVICTED murderer.

Lisa served seven years in prison for shooting and killing her father. Her dad was an alcoholic and very abusive. When he was a young boy, his mother allowed men to come in and out of his life who abused him, teaching him that this was normal and acceptable. As he grew into adulthood, he used alcohol as a measure to abuse Lisa and her mother. Lisa and her mom were somehow able to shelter Lisa's younger sisters from her father's abusive ways. She was the oldest child and felt it was her responsibility to make sure everyone was kept safe.

To be certain, her father did awful things to her—as did her maternal grandfather.

The first time Lisa can remember being hit was around nine years old. She was begging her father to stop beating her mother when he turned on her. Her father hit her so hard, her face bruised almost immediately.

From that day on, Lisa was filled with fear.

He then began selling her for sex. He physically beat and emotionally tormented Lisa. Although she lived in fear of her father, she also spent her childhood as the fierce protector for the family.

If her father was late for supper, she knew he'd likely come home drunk and angry and would lash out at her or her mom. Whenever he would come home late, just as he'd walk in the front door, Lisa would gather up her sisters and she and her mom would head out the back door to avoid any conflict. They'd pile into the family car, where her mom kept a bag of blankets hidden in the trunk. They'd drive toward the nearest church or a grocery store parking lot, where they would spend the night hiding so he wouldn't beat the hell out of them.

Her childhood was akin to living through a war, one she learned to live with until she simply could take no more pain and abuse. Since childhood, she had been shot at with automatic weapons and chased down by tractor trailers. She even hid her siblings under the house when she thought her dad was going to drive his truck right through the living room. The list of abuses—and shocking ones, at that—was endless.

On the day her father died, he put a gun in Lisa's face and told her he was going to get rid of the worst mistake he had ever made. At the time, she was nineteen years old and had endured ten years of unfathomable violence. That day, Lisa knew someone was going to die. It would either be her or her father. And others knew it, too, including her father who told relatives he was going to kill her or she was going to kill him. Either way, one of them would end up dead.

To this day, Lisa doesn't remember going to get a gun or how she loaded it. She had never used a gun before, but, somehow, she loaded and cocked it. Then she shot her dad and killed him.

The next thing she can recall is being arrested. She had no idea her father was dead and refused to believe anyone saying he was. They charged her with second-degree murder and use of a firearm in the commission of a felony. Her mother testified against her, saying Lisa told her to take the kids to the back of the house because she was going to kill her father. They would have tried to make a first-degree murder charge stick, but Lisa had no recollection of the moments leading up to her father's death or the actual shooting.

The prison placed Lisa in solitary confinement, where she spent most of her incarceration because she refused to eat. She also refused to take bond because she genuinely thought her dad was still alive and would retaliate against her. When she finally accepted that he was really dead, there was no relief in knowing what she had done.

Lisa was sentenced to a total of twenty-two years—twenty years for second-degree murder and two years for the gun charge. She was released after seven years, though she had been turned down for parole several times before due to the violent nature of her crime.

Throughout the years, police and Child Protective Services had been called to help her family, but they refused to do anything to assist or relieve the family. Every time they investigated the situation, they could find no reason to remove the children from the home because they never saw the father do anything themselves. They couldn't or wouldn't take Lisa's, her mother's, or the other kids' word. It didn't matter if Lisa was bleeding or had bruises all over her face and body. The authorities told her they'd have to see the act or there was nothing they could do. The last time they came to the house, they threatened Lisa's mother that they'd take her kids away if they were called to the home again. This instilled both fear and the belief that the government would not protect them. Lisa, her mother, and her siblings were victims of the system every bit as much as they were at the hands of their abuser.

The abuse Lisa endured in her home and at the hands of the system was horrific and, sadly, very common. Of course, the abuse wasn't Lisa's fault, though she still carries a great deal of guilt. She now understands that her father was part of a cycle that started with the abuse he endured as a child. He didn't know anything different. His aggressive behavior was normal to him and carried into his role as a parent. But Lisa also knew the cycle needed to stop. In Lisa's eyes, since the authorities wouldn't help, the only way to make the abuse stop was to shoot her father dead.

The sad reality is that nineteen-year-old Lisa and the people of the United States are in the same position. We have been abused by the government and we can't call anyone for help. Not a soul is coming to help. The Constitution gave us the authority to kill this government and start over if it usurped power from the people.

We are very close to that reality now. And we are being forced into the same shoes as a desperate and scared Lisa, knowing that no matter what choice we make, it will be wrought with pain and sacrifice.

The abusive relationship we find ourselves in with our government is an aspect of the loss of liberty that is not often talked about. The classic hallmarks of an abusive relationship involve a spouse who is controlling. Here's what I mean: An abusive spouse controls your money, restricts your movement, restricts your associations with other people, and threatens to harm you. An abusive spouse threatens your health and well-being your children, your property, and your freedom. And that's exactly what we've been living with under the oppression of our own government. The government controls our money, it restricts our movement, it restricts our associations with other people, and it threatens us with harm. It threatens our health and well-being it fails to protect our children, it can confiscate our property, and it denies us our God-given freedoms.

More and more each day, we are living in an abusive relationship with our federal, state, and local governments.

"*She fell. I didn't lay a hand on her.*"
"*She was going crazy and I had to hit her to get her attention.*"
"*I mean, it's really her fault.*"
"*She asked for it.*"

This is the narrative police across the United States hear every day when responding to domestic violence calls. It's also exactly what the nation heard from the police in Buffalo, New York, on June 4, 2020:

"*He tripped and fell.*"

That was the original response of the Buffalo Police Department when asked about Martin Gugino, the seventy-five-year-old peaceful protester they forcibly knocked to the ground in June 2020. We all saw the video footage that clearly showed that police force was used, sending Gugino to the pavement, where he hit his head and lay bleeding from his ears. None of the police officers stopped to help. They kept marching forward, moving the crowd along their path and leaving Gugino all alone.

Two officers, Robert McCabe and Aaron Torgalski, were initially suspended without pay, prompting dozens of fellow officers to step down from Buffalo's Emergency Response Team unit in protest. Buffalo District Attorney John Flynn admitted that the officers crossed the line, and McCabe and Torgalski were arrested and charged with second-degree assault. In New York, if the victim is age sixty-five or older and the perpetrator is ten years younger, the assault is automatically a felony charge. Even so, both officers were released without bail. If you or I knocked the same man down, we would have been charged with felony aggravated assault and battery and likely held and only released with bail.

In the days and weeks that followed the death of George Floyd, we saw continued and unconscionable abuse by our government and police force, over and over.

Isn't that exactly what you'd expect from a domestic abuser?

Over the course of my career, I have worked with many people who have been victims or have been charged with domestic violence. The first time someone gets hit, it's a shock. They love this person and he/she hit them? How can that be love? What I have observed in nearly every case is that the abuser truly believes that the ends justify the means. If you are willing to physically hurt someone you love to get them to do what you want, then what you want must be so important that you're willing to make that sacrifice.

I want to give you another example that makes my case. However, I must warn you: it's an immigration case, and I'm sure with the politization of immigration, a certain number of readers will have an initial negative reaction to the fact that the victim is an immigrant. Not only is she an immigrant, but she is a mother, a human being with inherent worth, and she cares about her child just as we care about ours. She is us, and we are her.

I serve immigrants every day because, like other people I serve, they get shoved to the margins. I want to ask you to take the politics of immigration out of this story. Genuinely compassionate conservatives should see that people like this are a natural new expansion of conservative ideology, based on the concept of individual liberty and core conservative values.

Beata Mejia-Mejia is a fiercely brave woman from Guatemala who was escaping abuse in her home country. In June 2018, the civil rights law firm I fund, Nexus Derechos Humanos (NDH), filed a case on behalf of Beata, who was seeking asylum in the United States. Her husband, Macario, was a police officer and a known gang member in Guatemala, where police moonlighting as gangsters is not uncommon. Beata's husband had taken a younger lover whom he wanted to marry.

Throughout their relationship, Beata was consistently beaten, raped, verbally assaulted, and mentally abused by Macario. Based on her asylum interview, which Trump government officials found to be credible, when Beata's husband found someone new, his decision wasn't just to leave her, it was to kill her and their seven-year-old son, Darwin. This meant they'd no longer be his responsibility, and Macario would be free and clear to move on.

Although domestic violence can mean many different things, it is usually understood as a threat or the infliction of physical harm by one person onto another in a family or home. By definition, a household is a group of people who live together, whether or not they are related by blood, marriage, or adoption.

The Immigration and Naturalization Act states that one could qualify for asylum in the US if they have been (or if they fear they will be) persecuted in their home country either by their government or by persons or groups that their government is unwilling or unable to control because of their political opinion, religion, race, nationality, or membership in a particular social group.

If that person can prove they are a victim of domestic violence, they may, under limited circumstances, be eligible for asylum—that is, provided that the violence perpetrated against them is motivated by one of the five grounds mentioned above, and that their government is unwilling or unable to protect them from the perpetrator. Beata met these conditions in multiple ways and that is why her hearing to receive asylum was determined to be credible.

In August 2014, a landmark decision became one of the most important precedents for asylum cases. The Board of Immigration Appeals (BIA) issued *Matter of A-R-C-G,* a ruling that approved asylum to a woman from Guatemala because of the serious abuse she endured from her spouse.[3] During her testimony, the woman spoke about how her husband beat her weekly, burned her with paint thinner, and raped her. Even though she contacted the Guatemalan police many times, they refused to get involved because they "would not interfere in a marital relationship." The BIA found that this woman qualified for asylum as a victim of domestic violence, holding that "married women in Guatemala who are unable to leave their relationship" can represent a particular social group that forms the basis of a claim for asylum or withholding of removal.

Like this woman, Beata escaped her abusive home and fled to America with the hope of starting over. However, when she arrived, she and Darwin were met by ICE, where they were instantly separated and became victims of the family separation tragedy in this country. This woman had already suffered unimaginable abuse. Her only conceivable recourse was to seek asylum in the United States, and how did our country treat her?

Exactly the same as her husband had.

She had escaped that hell in Guatemala to come to the United States, where she instantly found herself living in a different type of hell no parent should ever have to experience—being forcibly separated from their children.

To me, this treatment seems unfair. To Beata, it is exactly what she expected. She had no trust in anyone, especially a government, not even ours. She had just come out of an abusive relationship with a man who worked for a government that she lived under and who worked for the gangs he was supposed to be policing. He was totally corrupt. The similarities Beata dealt with from her abusive husband and what she dealt with from the United States government are very clear. Her parental rights and the concern for her child were inhumanely ignored. When she was separated from her child, Beata had to watch strangers in government uniforms lead her son away, knowing she might never see him again. She was taunted, saying she was a bad mother and if she never saw her son again, it was what she deserved. The reality was, all she was doing was fighting to save her son's life.

After her release, the government held her son, claiming she needed to go through an elongated sponsorship process designed for strangers who adopt a child in the immigration system. The government knew Beata was weak and hopeless and burdened, just like her husband had believed. However, she did not lose hope. She fled her husband to save her own life and that of her son. And with my help through Nexus Derechos Humanos, she fought the attorney general and the president of the United States, and she won.

Beata and her son, Darwin, are now happily living in Texas.

Sadly, another example of how our government abuses its citizens can be found in the way we treat children in our juvenile justice system. Every day, children across this country who are in the justice system face solitary confinement, shackling, pepper spray, restraints, and physical and sexual abuse. Many of them face being pepper-sprayed for disobeying rules, strip-searched after family visits, and shackled by their wrists and ankles when they leave their cells. When a child is sent to confinement, he or she may be locked in a cell as small as seven-by-ten feet, sometimes twenty-two to twenty-four hours per day. When that happens, they are denied access to their personal belongings, educational services, necessary counseling, and mental-health treatment. On top of that, they have zero interaction with peers. Often the cell is barren, usually with only a lightly padded concrete slab to sleep on. These children, simply put, are treated like caged and abused animals.

The extraordinarily harsh conditions and practices in our youth prisons can easily interfere with normal child development, lead to trauma, and worsen pre-existing physical and emotional disabilities. The long-term impact of solitary confinement and barbaric practices such as strip searches can and often does lead to a lifelong struggle of feeling worthless, humiliated, and ashamed. And then there are the kids who have already suffered some form of sexual abuse prior to entering the system. They are the most vulnerable to being retraumatized, especially by the strip searches. The psychological impact can be so severe that it is not unusual for these kids to self-harm or attempt suicide, either during their detention or later in life due to enduring psychosis. Although federal law explicitly prohibits sexual violence against incarcerated youth and adults, children are considered high risk of sexual assault in both juvenile and adult facilities.

And it happens—a lot.

Solitary confinement is, without a doubt, one of the most destructive and counterproductive practices that occurs in juvenile justice facilities. With no known benefits, thousands of youths under the age of eighteen are subjected to solitary confinement in juvenile facilities across America. It's widely known that black and brown kids, LGBTQ, gender non-conforming, and those with disabilities are more likely to be placed in solitary confinement, which administrators sometimes justify as necessary, "for their own protection," or because the facility lacks appropriate services or accommodations.

Those who oversee juveniles in the justice system have a basic responsibility to ensure the safety and security of those in their care. According to the *Journal of the American Academy of Psychiatry and the Law*, solitary confinement is a form of child abuse that can and often does cause long-term psychological and emotional harm, trauma, depression, anxiety, and increased risk of self-harm. It can also increase mental illness and post-traumatic stress responses experienced by many kids in the juvenile justice system. Sadly, more than half of youth who commit suicide inside facilities do so in solitary confinement.

Because of limited resources, facility administrators and staff often use solitary confinement for youth with unaddressed mental health, behavioral, or developmental needs. Because youth in solitary confinement don't have access to behavioral health services, education, and treatment, solitary confinement undermines the very purpose of juvenile justice facilities—rehabilitation.

In 2019, Nexus Derechos Humanos had a case in New York (*Paykina v. Lewin*) where the client had been incarcerated since he was fifteen years old.[4] At seventeen, he was transferred to Albany, New York, where he was placed at the Hudson Correctional Facility and held in solitary confinement, including a barbaric ten-day, twenty-four-hour-a-day stretch. Solitary confinement is the involuntary placement of a youth alone in a cell, room, or other area for any reason other than as a temporary response to behavior that threatens immediate physical harm. Most youth facilities refer to solitary confinement by different names—seclusion, isolation, segregation, or room confinement. As nice as room confinement may sound, the effects are devastating. I sometimes send my kids to their room, but their room isn't a concrete slab to sleep on with a toilet to drink out of. It has internet, a comfortable mattress, and windows.

The young man we represented had a history of mental health challenges and was known to be violent. He most likely needed interdiction and support, but he certainly didn't need to be abused by the system. The prison subjected our client to unusually long periods of deprivation at the prison, where his access to water, showers, food, and social interaction was severely restricted. His conditions in the Adolescent Offender Segregation Unit were so bad that he reacted with self-mutilating behavior, cutting himself on the arm as a cry for help. This cruel punishment went on for seven months. He was held alone in an eight-and-a-half-by-ten-foot cell, leaving only four hours a day on weekdays and two hours on weekends. During those hours away from his cell, he was handcuffed. He spent his "recreation" time alone in a cage.

Youth in confinement are already in a fragile mental state. After hearing about his confinement, we got a court order to inspect his cell. When we arrived, we found the words, "I need a doctor" on the wall, written with crayon, food, and bodily excrement. The plea was visible from the window in the cell door, but no one would help.

If that's not child abuse, what is?

Our suit went after Governor Andrew Cuomo and State Attorney General Letitia James, because it was our belief that they were responsible for such horrific abuse. Here's why. It wasn't Elliot Spitzer and Eric Schneiderman's New York anymore where both politicians abused their power for their own personal gain, ultimately committing crimes they were prosecuting people for at the same time. Things were supposed to be different when Letitia James, the new attorney general, took the helm. She was an advocate in New York City and supported the elimination of solitary confinements for juveniles. She railed about juvenile solitary confinement when it was the side of the law she wanted to protect. And now, she was sending lawyers to the same courts to say the state has an absolute right and need to confine our seventeen-year-old client in solitary? This was hypocrisy and abuse at its worst.

Thankfully, US District Judge Brenda Sannes agreed with our complaint and entered a groundbreaking injunction that said the state of New York could not hold him in solitary confinement anymore. She cited his severe isolation as a major factor in his deteriorating mental health. While the young man was returned to the general population in a different upstate New York prison to serve out the rest of his sentence, his life was forever and irreversibly changed by his experiences in solitary confinement.

Our client's case is just one example of how these practices are cruel and incredibly damaging to the kids who are placed in solitary. We want to stop any practice that meets this definition, regardless of what it is labeled or how it is explained away. Solitary confinement doesn't work, and it undercuts the primary goal of facility administrators and staff who employ it—to preserve the safety and security of an institution.

Think about everything I've now shared with you about solitary confinement. Now think about what would happen if you treated your children the same way. If you locked your child in a barren room for twenty-two hours a day, refused to educate him, and beat him when he talked back to you, the result would be that you would lose your child and go to jail. Who would you lose your child to? Who would put you in jail? The very same people who are abusing children in that same system. This is surely a double standard, but it's worse than just that. It's malevolent abuse, and its representative of the same "ends justify the means" philosophy that has brought the United States to the brink of civil war.

Some states, such as New Jersey, have made progress in this area. In June 2019, thanks to the efforts of US Senator Cory Booker, New Jersey Governor Phil Murphy signed into law legislation that limits solitary confinement and bans the practice for vulnerable populations in state prisons. Senator Booker said, "Solitary confinement is torture. It is an archaic, damaging, and inefficient practice that has been proven to have irreversible effects. Yet, thousands of Americans are held in isolation daily. As a nation founded on the principle of liberty and justice for all, this practice is wholly unjust and leaves the incarcerated worse off. It is my sincere hope that lawmakers around the country follow New Jersey's leadership to ensure their corrections systems are more humane and use proven methods to rehabilitate incarcerated individuals."[5] Senator Booker is right; however, New Jersey boasts an arrest rate for black citizens that is twelve times that of its white citizens. Hypocrisy and double standards will never solve this problem.

Other states around the country have introduced or passed legislation to limit solitary confinement for youth, and a growing number of states now face federal litigation for using solitary confinement on young people.

Youth corrections systems in Ohio, Indiana, Massachusetts, and Oregon have improved the safety of facilities and decreased violence involving youth and staff by reducing the use of solitary confinement. The Massachusetts Department of Youth Services rarely uses solitary confinement for more than one hour and does not use solitary confinement as punishment. Other states and local jurisdictions have also taken steps to reform the use of juvenile solitary confinement on youth. Some efforts have taken the form of agency policy change or statewide legislation, while others have been in response to litigation and legislation, some of which I have funded. Still, there are too many states that haven't joined this movement toward eliminating solitary confinement for our youth, i.e. government child abuse.

On the federal level, in late 2018, legislation with bipartisan support passed the First Step Act, which limits the use of solitary confinement for youth in federal custody. The Office of Juvenile Justice and Delinquency Prevention (OJJDP) strongly supports efforts to end youth solitary. The reauthorized Juvenile Justice and Delinquency Prevention Act (JJDPA) will require OJJDP to collect data on the use of solitary in youth facilities and actions states are taking to limit its use. Many professional organizations including the American Academy of Adolescent and Child Psychiatry, the American Psychological Association, the National Partnership for Juvenile Services, the American Bar Association, and the National Council of Juvenile and Family Court Judges support the end of solitary confinement for youth.

Still asking whether we might be in an abusive relationship with our government?

As in any abusive relationship, when it comes to our government, if you are good, follow the rules, and don't cause any problems, you're less likely to get hit. But if you're annoying to the elites, like I can be, you get hit all the time. We want to believe the government keeps us safe. Just like a victim who wants to believe she won't get hit again, we convince ourselves that if we just take it *this time* it will get better. It won't, of course, without America returning to a foundation of a principle of individual liberty. The police state will always abuse us. Power is control, and "total domination," in the words of President Trump, is exactly what the police state demands.

Think about money and control. The more abusive the relationship is, the less money we get to keep. How many times have you felt that it's unfair that your money goes into a giant ubiquitous pot and you don't know what it's functionally doing? Just look at your last paycheck or tax returns—I am sure you will get what I am saying. We've all had those frustrations. While I don't think it's unfair to tax people, the government taxes us and penalizes us with the idea that your money is needed for the common good. "Okay," we say. "But then we don't get a say in the process?" "No," they say. "You don't." Is that about control? Perhaps. Security? Your government certainly wants you living in the middle of that paper, believing they are caring for you. And it's definitely about any number of things the government wants to push, whether it's in your best interest or not. It's just more "Meet the new boss, same as the old boss."

In a post-COVID society, we have even seen government restrictions on how and where you can spend your money. If you're a business owner, you couldn't open to make money, pay your employees, and stay afloat. And as a citizen, you were restricted by the closed economy. This is so much like a relationship with a domestic abuser who won't allow his wife to leave the house or have friends of her own. When things are running smoothly, everything is fine. But as soon as you have a situation where they're set off, there is upheaval before an apology. And with that apology, everything is supposed to be better. One of the best examples of how this shows up in our government today is with the George Floyd murder. The government, city and state, and police officials who are liberal democrats don't understand why when the Minneapolis police chief removed his hat and took a knee while talking to the family it didn't resolve their problems. And why would this act of "apology" resolve the tension?

That's *exactly* what government expects from us. They want an easy resolutione. It really doesn't matter the ideology of the government, because, no matter what, that government will fight to survive.

But...will you?

Most of us believe we would never stay in a relationship with someone who abuses us. But many do. They justify the behavior in ways that make it easier to stay than leave. But if you allow that behavior to continue, you will most likely get hit again and again, which means your circumstances only get worse.

The governments control over our lives is all-expansive, telling us what we can and cannot do, when, where, and with whom. We all live in one of the most documented examples of an abusive relationship, and we assume that we don't have a choice.

Why?

What other choice do we have?

That's the same gut-wrenching call abused spouses make every day. Truly, we are all abused.

Our governments are commanding us to stand back up and toe the line.

That's certainly one approach. Another is to hit back and hit back hard, right? To fight like your life depends on it. If you don't, chronic abuse becomes your new normal. Check that. Not new. Just normal. Are you really okay with that?

My oldest son, Sam, is now at an age where he is dating. When I counsel him on relationships, I explain that when he and his girlfriend have fights, sometimes he might say something he later regrets, like, "I hate you." And once he goes there, it becomes the expectation, the norm that whenever they fight, this is what he will say. And you don't come back from that because you went there.

Our government went there with us. Only when they did, they took a step back and basically asked, "Now, what are you going to do about it?"

It doesn't take a PhD to know that answer. Sometimes you simply have to stand up for yourself. If you don't, you lose the ability to do so. What becomes of you is whatever the entity that's hurting you wants you to become. You have given that person, that government, all of the control.

We have a government that takes our most precious commodities away from us—time, relationships, freedom, and liberties. But what is the government afraid of? What terrifies the abuser the most? When you think about it, the abuser isn't terrified of losing the person they're abusing because they know that person is there and likely not leaving. What terrifies the abuser is the awakening of that person. They're petrified that someone will reach them, and that person will finally have enough courage to change their circumstances.

Isn't that exactly what our government is afraid of?

When you see tens of thousands of people—black, brown, white, and yellow—funneling into the streets to protest, the government's response, just like a domestic abuser, is to say, "I'm sorry. We won't do that again."

Is that supposed to make us feel better?

Are we really supposed to believe that's the solution?

Many of us believe we are not at risk, but we are. We just live in a community of privilege. The enforcing arms of the government aren't reaching you because you're not the target. But what happens when you are? Shelley Luther became a symbol of conservative outrage over the Texas state lockdown and stay-at-home orders for non-essential businesses to stay closed when she opened her hair salon during the coronavirus pandemic. When served with a cease-and-desist letter sent to her by local authorities, she refused and subsequently ripped it up. Luther kept her salon open, defying orders to close. As a result, she was taken into custody and fined $3,500 for ignoring a temporary restraining order that prohibited her business from operating.

At her hearing, Eric Moye, the civil district judge of Dallas presiding over her case, said he thought the decision to open her salon was "selfish" and requested an apology. Luther took great exception to the judge's claim, explaining that making a choice to feed her kids wasn't selfish; it was survival. Unsatisfied, the judge found her in contempt of court and ordered her to a week in jail and to pay a $7,000 fine. State Attorney General Ken Paxton urged the judge to reconsider and immediately released Luther, saying Moye had abused his discretion by ordering her to jail. Paxton's request was met with tremendous criticism by other judges from Dallas County saying it violated the Texas Code of Judicial Conduct.

But Paxton may have had a personal reason for wanting Shelley Luther freed. In 2015, even though Ken Paxton was the most powerful attorney in Texas, he was indicted on three felony securities fraud charges. Yet Paxton was not jailed. In other words, the person in charge of managing the law in Texas was innocent until proven guilty, so why should Shelley Luther have gone to jail?

It's all so arbitrary.

Everyone in charge of this case seems to have behaved inappropriately: The governor created the executive order that said Luther could be jailed. The judge overstepped in his decision to sentence Luther to serve time because she was in contempt. Even Texas Governor Greg Abbot later said, "Throwing Texans in jail who have had their businesses shut down through no fault of their own is nonsensical." Incensed, the governor modified his executive orders calling for violators to either pay a fine or serve up to 180 days in jail and retroactively removed confinement as punishment for violating the lockdown. The State Supreme Court agreed, ordering her released on a personal bond, with no money required, pending final disposition of her case.

Within hours, Shelley Luther was free to leave.

At first glance, this story may seem to be nothing more than a flagrant publicity stunt for all involved, but it brings up several obvious hypocritical decisions that were made by the most powerful people running that state of Texas. By standing her ground and fighting for her rights, Luther became a hero of sorts to conservatives for defying the officials that wielded the power to incarcerate her in the first place. Texas Republicans demanded her immediate release. The lieutenant governor of Texas even offered to place himself on house arrest to help free her. He also gave her the $7,000 to pay her fine.

Underlying the entire story is a reaffirmation of what government *is* in the United States and, perhaps more important, what it *isn't*. See, the government makes laws and then selectively punishes violators. The more money and power you have, the more you can get away with.

It's critical that you understand the government is not your friend, not your partner, and not your parent. If you make the government angry, the government will come after you. And when they do, as we saw with Shelley Luther, they will come hard and they won't care how much they hurt you or what else they destroy in the process.

The government will always protect money and power, and the government will always attempt to maintain control.

Our government provides what I refer to as a "privilege push." This is where most Americans are left alone so the government can focus on the most undesirable people, which includes the black and brown communities and those in poor white communities. For example, according to CNN and ProPublica, 80 percent of the arrests in New York City for stay-at-home order violations were of black and brown people. In Cincinnati and the majority of the surrounding areas, the arrests in the African-American community hovered around 79 percent during the stay-at-home orders. And in Texas, aside from Luther, two other women, Ana Isabel Castro-Garcia and Brenda Stephanie Mata, were also arrested for offering nail and eyelash services from their homes. This violated the Laredo emergency management plan. Both faced misdemeanor charges and up to 180 days in jail. The governor wanted to make sure these women didn't suffer the same injustice Luther did. He made a valid point when he said, "As some county judges advocate for releasing hardened criminals from jail to prevent the spread of COVID-19, it is absurd to have these business owners take their place."

Indeed.

Look, if your partner hits you and then they apologize and you forgive and forget, is it your fault when you get hit again?

Absolutely not. It's a disease and you're a victim of it, but knowing that, is it possible you could have done something proactively and objectively to change the outcome?

Yes.

And that's exactly where we are in this country. We are battered women and men—victims of our own government—and we now know it. We've seen it and felt it, which is why it matters now more than ever. If we can't find the courage to get out, then this is what the relationship is going to be like forever.

We can't let that happen to the greatest democratic experiment the world has ever seen. We just can't.

We can no longer permit this abuse.

3

CONVICTED

My name is Mike Donovan, and I am a convicted felon.

For those like me, that always matters first and, usually, is all that matters. While I have felony convictions, they do not define me, and I don't let them control me. I am informed and inspired by the experiences I've had, which make me a better person every day. I am proud of my convictions, both those built through an incredible faith in God and those handed down by a corrupt and exploitive criminal-justice system.

I grew up in Briery Branch, a mountain community in far western Virginia not far from Dayton. Dayton is known for its "old order" Mennonite community, which meant that horses and carriages were as common as cars. It was an entirely white community and, consequently, historically racist.

I remember as a child an incident where African-American visitors had been blocked from proceeding on the highway by individuals who rolled a dumpster onto the road to prevent them from passing though. Someone had spray-painted the N-word on the dumpster, which, even at my very young age, I found particularly disgusting. My most vivid memory of this incident wasn't the act itself though. It was that no one else in the community other than my mom and dad were revolted by the act. I realized that I was being raised differently than everybody else. At the time, I didn't understand why or the impact this would have as I got older.

My family lived in a converted one-room schoolhouse apartment. If you don't know what that is, these were turn-of-the-century K–12 schools that were converted to apartment buildings. Each classroom was turned into an individual apartment. It was very small, no more than 800 square feet. Despite living in such a cramped space, we somehow found ways to make it work. We didn't have a lot. My dad worked all the time and was rarely home. He was a very hard worker. As a kid, I watched him work two and three jobs, sleeping just a few hours a night. It is amazing how much my life today has mirrored his example. His work ethic inspired me to do things for other people in this life, and I will forever credit him with that.

Dad was a good provider, making sure my mom, brothers, and I always had food to eat and medical care whenever we needed it. When my dad had a good month at work, he might have found himself with an extra ten or twenty dollars, which he always put toward what he referred to as his "life or death" bills. Once in a while, my brother and I could go to McDonald's or Burger King, but those days were very few and far between. Some of my friends went to Red Lobster. On a special occasion, we went to Arby's. I knew my parents didn't have any money, and I never asked for more than my dad could provide. Dad tried to be a stabilizing figure even though we struggled. He never sugarcoated our circumstances, offering the perception that things were better than they were. He believed in seeing the truth, knowing the truth, and understanding that life is hard—and to expect it to be that way. He always told me that it's better to be expecting the worst and experience a pleasant surprise than it is to expect the best and then be perpetually disappointed. I appreciated my father for teaching me this as a young boy.

I was a smart kid, but I didn't realize every kid didn't think the way I did. I stood out. I was trying to figure out what made me different, especially why my parents' values were different from my friends' parents. I quickly learned that value systems aren't necessarily wrong. I learned that you can disagree on something, but both ideas can be passionately held.

I was the first in my family to go to college. By the fall of 1998, I'd set off to Northern Virginia. During my first semester at school, a group of friends and I decided to spend the weekend at the Crystal City Marriott. When my friend's credit card was declined, I asked the front desk if I could cash two checks for seven hundred dollars to cover the cost of the rooms. They obliged, and I paid with the cash.

We stayed and enjoyed our weekend.

Yes, I knew I didn't have the money in my account to cover the amount they were written for. I am not saying what I did was justifiable in any way. But I was young, and I wasn't thinking about the consequences. I remember thinking I'd be able to come up with the money before the checks hit the bank Monday morning.

At the time in Virginia, if you wrote a bad check and it was over $200, you could be charged with three separate felonies: the "uttering" of the check, which is the act of handing it over to someone; forgery, which is signing it and saying there was money to cover the amount knowing there wasn't; and grand larceny, which is tied to the goods and/or services received.

You might say it was a little aggressive for the state to charge three different ways for something like a bad check, but that's how prosecutors influence the creation of law. It's also how they get plea bargains. Since I had written two checks, there were a total of six felonies I was initially arrested for.

When I was picked up for this crime, an imposing grandfather type introduced himself as Detective Griswold. He was quick to tell me that I was going to learn an important lesson, and that it would be a *really* hard one. At the time, I remember thinking he was just being arrogant and trying to scare me. He certainly laid it on thick with the magistrate judge (a judicial officer in Virginia who holds initial bail hearings), telling him they were conducting a full investigation. He pleaded with the magistrate judge to keep me in jail until they had more information. They were looking into whether or not I had passed any other bad checks, especially in the surrounding areas of Maryland and DC. While I can vividly remember hearing those words, I was shocked and in a state of panic, and I was left frozen and unable to defend myself in that moment.

The judge set my bond at $45,500, an amount of money I just couldn't imagine.

I knew my mom and dad couldn't help. They had no savings and nothing to put up as collateral. My dad tried to get a loan to come up with the 10 percent bond but wasn't able to secure one. At the time, I had hoped their efforts would be successful, but I knew this was my responsibility—my fight. My life was about to get real context.

So I sat there in my cell, alone and afraid.

Up until my arrest, my dream was to become a lawyer. Now I had to reconcile that I had probably messed that up over a foolish, poor choice.

I found out by walking through the fire that life is all about choices.

The decision I made to write those checks would shape every aspect of my life going forward, from my career to my advocacy work. It was hard to understand in the moment, but looking back, I realize now there's simply no way I would have found my calling without walking through that fire.

In my first twenty-four hours of being incarcerated, I saw and had things happen to me that were hard to speak about for many years. I wasn't as strong back then as I am today. If they were trying to scare me, it worked. I remember thinking I was going to die in that roach-infested hell hole—that this would be where I spent the remaining days of my life. Admittedly that was a bit dramatic. It was one lesson about context I learned hard and fast—that my fear was based on a false promise that as an American I was innocent until proven guilty. Most of the black and brown people I met in jail had a different context, and their lives had led them to no expectation that their rights would be protected—or that those rights even existed.

Before my first court date, I told George Gills, my court-appointed attorney, to do whatever he could to get me out of there. "Make a deal," I begged him. "I'll plead guilty. I don't care as long as I don't have to stay inside the system."

What I quickly learned was many convicted felons didn't commit the crimes they were accused of. Like me, they just gave in to the process. While there are some public defenders who really care about their clients, even those are ridiculously overworked and overwhelmed. Many more just don't care about the outcome. All they want to do is get your case off their ever-expanding pile of things to do. While I appreciated the work my public defender was doing, and I have a great deal of respect for him now, he wasn't a die-on-your-sword defense attorney. He was practical. "Mike, you are going to spend about a year in jail," I remember him saying. Basically, what he was saying was, "Get over it." While he wasn't Johnny Cochran for me in my case, he taught me a lot about the challenges of the public-defender system that have shaped the pro bono work I do to this day.

Over the next few days, I kept getting called down to the booking desk. Each time I appeared, there were new warrants from all over Virginia. I had warrants from cities I'd never even been to—and they were all bad-check warrants.

Now, this was in the days before the internet that connected everyone in law enforcement. Instead, they had a teletype report that would be sent out after an arrest to gather additional information if law enforcement felt there might have been other instances in surrounding communities. When Griswold sent out my report, he didn't say my name was Micheal Donovan, which is how I spell my name. He said that was a pseudonym. He wrote, AKA Michael Donovan, Mike Donovan, Mickey Donovan, and every other derivative and spelling imaginable. That meant anybody who had written a similar dollar amount check that looked like me, white, 180 pounds, approximately eighteen years old, was a match. I got sent as a possible suspect to thirty different police stations all over Virginia because of the way they put the description into the system.

In my head, I kept hearing Detective Griswold say, "You're going to learn a lesson and it's going to be a hard one," every time I was cuffed, put in the back of a patrol car, and sent to another jail.

Jail is horrible but when you have to go from one jail to another, it's a constant and unnecessary threat. At least it was for me. Sometimes I was placed in the drunk tank for weeks, awaiting a hearing. Other times I was placed in a general containment unit, a very heavily supervised place in jail that's on twenty-three-hour-a-day lockdown. It was terrifying.

I found myself in places I'd never been, defending myself against a crime I didn't commit. Sometimes there would be a witness there who could clear me, someone who could easily say, "That's not the guy." So they'd have to drop the charges. Other times, I wasn't as lucky.

By the time I went before the judge in Arlington, which was where my legitimate charges were being heard, my attorney said that since I had already pleaded guilty to the six felonies I was being charged with, the court would sentence me to time served. If, however, I didn't want to plead guilty, the judge was going to order me to eight months in a detention/diversion "boot camp," a hardcore prison work camp. If that wasn't bad enough, the wait in jail to get into the program would have been one to three years. None of that time would have counted, and I would have just been sitting in jail as if time had stopped. The presiding judge over my case was one of the visionaries of the work camp and was extremely proud of the program's success. If the prosecutor asked for that sentence, the judge always said yes.

Virginia no longer offers that program, but they did then. And while it had its merit, it wasn't what I needed. And they knew that.

I want to be very clear: I was guilty of the original charges. I should have served time for what I did. But charging me with six felonies was not right.

When you're young, naïve, and scared, when you're working with court-appointed counsel, and when you don't understand the system, you are very willing to take whatever you must to get credit for time served and get out.

In the end, I spent eight months behind bars and came out a multi-time *convicted* felon. With each additional warrant and dismissal representing another entry on my criminal record, my record at first glance looks more like a novel than a computer printout. It isn't until you read it that you see the vast majority of those charges were dismissed.

Unfortunately, once the system marks you, you're branded for life.

I also came out of that experience knowing I needed to make a difference for others who found themselves in the same place I'd just been. I had a lot of time to think during those eight months. Just like I did when I was kid, I spent a great amount of my time trying to understand why different people are treated differently and why so many act in a different way.

Up until my incarceration, I'd only experienced prison the way most of you reading this book have: by watching movies. I hadn't given it much thought. But my eyes became wide open from knowledge I left prison with. For eight months, I ate my meals as one of the only white men in the jail. For the most part, every single guy in line was black or brown. It was shocking to me because it didn't make any sense. I wanted to understand why that was. So I got to know the guys, asking them questions, allowing myself to become educated on why they were being treated differently than I was.

While the privilege I had as a young white man was certainly broken by being incarcerated, there's no question that my privilege still existed. Once I was released, I would have the ability to get a job, find an apartment to rent, and not be seen as a dangerous person who didn't deserve another chance.

That's what white privilege is for convicted felons.

Most white Americans don't understand the African-American experience in this country. If a white man is pulled over in an upscale community, the first thing an officer says to him is something like, "Do you know you were speeding?" If a black man is pulled over in that same upscale community, the officer more likely says something like, "Put your hands where I can see them."

In the eyes of many, that lack of understanding of what it's like to be black in this country leads to being afraid of African Americans. That's a hard pill for many of us to swallow, but it's true. So when you add anything onto that irrational primal fear, you're destroying the ability of the African-American community to compete and thrive. The deck is stacked against them and has been for as long as America has been a country.

I've long understood that you can't just want things to be different. You actually have to do something to make a difference. Being a convicted felon certainly became one aspect of how the world would see me. And if I chose to allow that label to be placed on me and had accepted it, then that's exactly what the perception would be.

When you think about it, though, we are all convicted in one way or another. We are all "convicted" in a larger sense by something that holds us. Every mom is "convicted" by the love she feels for her child, every bit as much as you might feel "convicted" by witnessing something that should never have happened.

So while I have been convicted, I live convicted as well.

Running on the third wire of society would not have been where I saw myself growing up—no one sees themselves growing up that way—but I also know that is exactly who I was made to be. If the meekest and weakest have a shot in this world, then everybody does. If I don't fight for the meek when I can, who would be there to fight for me if the circumstances were reversed? In the words of the Jewish sage Rabbi Hillel, "If I am not for myself, who will be for me? And if I am only for myself, what am I? If not now, when?"

longer protective, so unless they are the ones wielding the weapons, the drugs, or other contraband, they're screwed.

Captain Arnold, Corporal Roth, and I created a model program that was then used across the country to help other jails figure out how to facilitate undercover operations. And through my own experience, I was given the opportunity to forge my own developing understanding of my calling. I had helped to catch dozens of guards committing crimes, but the system prosecuted only a couple. Through this, it became clear to me: that's privilege too.

It was after that experience that I realized I could go to law school. In fact, it was Captain Arnold who told me I could pursue that degree. Much to my surprise, he pointed out that one of the biggest criminal defense lawyers in Williamsburg is a convicted murderer. Upon hearing this, I enrolled in Western Governors University's four-year business law program. I decided that I wanted a degree with some legal foundation before attending law school. I finished my entire four-year program in five months using WGU's model, which allows students to take as many courses as they can and finish them as quickly as they are able. Using that model, I accomplished the seemingly impossible: I finished an entire four-year degree in almost as many months. After I finished the WGU program, I applied to law schools. I was accepted to the Charlotte School of Law and was offered a full-ride scholarship. It was a deal too good to pass up. I finished most of my degree work but never took my clinical courses or took the bar exam, which means I am not a practicing attorney.

My law school was part of the Infilaw Corporation, which operated a number of for-profit law schools. While people like me who received full scholarships made out great, the schools were known for churning through large numbers of students who would get stuck in mountains of debt. The Obama administration took aim at Infilaw and launched investigations. These investigations eventually forced the school to close. My schedule would not allow me to transfer to another school in what is called an American Bar Association "teach out" plan, where students of closed law schools can transfer and finish their degrees.

As a result, I never finished law school, and I am okay with that. Without a law degree, I have made a significant impact on the laws of this country by building and funding a team of lawyers who can do the work, and I am exceedingly proud of that.

I am proud to stand with these amazing people we serve, who are hardworking and fiercely committed to their families, and fight with them for a system that fosters their full inclusion in our society.

4

PRISON IS A MICROCOSM

PRISON IS A MICROCOSM OF SO MANY THINGS IN LIFE.

Imagine going through life being known by the worst thing you've ever done.

That's what happens when you go to prison. You are forced to live with the constant reminder of that mistake, because society never lets you forget. In many ways, that ongoing public perception is as if you are still serving time. I know that firsthand.

If you've never been in jail, you can't understand the feeling of having no control and losing your basic rights. You have to push a button and ask permission to do anything. I know what it's like to have no control over when I wake up and when I go to sleep. I know what it's like to have to ask permission to eat, to use the phone, to use the bathroom, to see a doctor, or merely to go outside.

When you think about it, we are all prisoners in one way or another. Maybe you are in a job you hate, maybe you're in a marriage you feel stuck in, or maybe you're living in a country that doesn't care about you or your needs.

While the perpetrator might serve a sentence, that person doesn't always pay the emotional toll of their actions. Victims of crime often struggle with anger, bitterness, or resentment for what they have gone through, carrying with them a different type of sentence, one they battle from within.

Even someone who struggles with a spiritual conflict can feel as confined by their choices as someone who lives in a five-by-eight cell. Fear, addiction, shame, and sin can imprison even the strongest of souls. Prison is a microcosm of that spiritual struggle too.

When I was an inmate, I was placed in a housing unit with seventy-eight men. In that unit, everything I did was under constant control by a concept called "direct supervision," meaning one guard is directly in charge of supervising fifty to one hundred inmates during his shift.

The traditional prison model is based on guards walking the catwalks and the prisoners living among themselves, left to their own devices. The guards only come in when they absolutely have to. Otherwise, the environment is run by prisoners. Over time, the concept of corrections in this country adapted to this idea of direct supervision. In theory, it means less violence and the guards can better control inmate behavior. Sometimes you have a nice guard, but not very often.

Why?

In my experience, nice guards never worked out in the system because the guys in the unit always knew how to work the nice guys for help: "I need help with my calls," "I need money for canteen," "Do I have any mail?" "Are you sure I don't have any mail?" It would be a never-ending barrage of "help me," until the guard simply could take no more.

The most effective guards were always some level of jerk. The rougher they were, the better they ran the unit. The theory was simple: the more afraid people were, the more controllable they were. If the guard led with fear, no one approached him. As a result, that guard's job was so much easier.

I was considered low risk in the housing unit where I was incarcerated. The crime of writing a bad check doesn't typically send you to a maximum-security unit, though as a relatively naïve kid, I thought I was heading to gladiator school. Luckily, the unit I lived in was minimum security and had one guard who was perhaps less trained and not as mean as a higher-risk unit guard. If you go to a housing unit where more people are undesirable to the prison warden, you're going to find meaner guards who are more aggressive.

Direct supervision was really meant as a way to make the prison environment safer for the operators of the prison. And so they placed individuals in control of large groups of people, making those people wholly dependent on those guards for of this crisis; we were just prolonging it. When a nanny thinks they know what's best for you, they tell you what to do. The American people don't need a nanny. Remember, sometimes nannies aren't the endearing and magical Mary Poppins. Quite the opposite, they can be abusive and deceiving. And that is what we saw in Manhattan and the outer boroughs during the quarantine when police officers beat on people or tased them for walking too close to others. Or in places like California, citations were handed out for walking on the beach or merely watching the sunset. That's what happens when you give the ultimate power to one person over another for something that is largely inconsequential. In California, Governor Newsom went so far as to create an executive order that said that only people who are family members can eat at the same table in a restaurant.

Really?

Since when does the state tell me who I can eat with or walk next to? It's like I am an employee instead of a free citizen. What's next? Asking permission to go to the bathroom? Asking if I can eat or drink? Wondering if I can give my son certain advice?

What rights do we really have at all in a nanny state? Whatever rights the nanny decides to confer at any given time? Remember, if they come from the state, they're not rights at all—they're privileges. Rights are God-given.

On the other hand, let's look at how the debate over wearing a mask during the pandemic went from being about health and safety to being about politics. How did wearing a mask become akin to the snake on the "Don't Tread on Me" posters and a sign of tyranny? I understand that the government has no right to enforce the wearing of a mask, but in the middle of a global pandemic, did it make sense for any of us not to wear one?

If you don't want to wear a mask during a pandemic, that should be your decision. But when you end up in a hospital during that pandemic, ask yourself, "Is my doctor wearing a left-wing tyrannical symbol on his face? Are the protective gloves he puts on before he sews up your open wound for your health or about his politics?"

Wearing masks should never have become about left-right politics. But the nanny state should never have had to legislate them. We all should have chosen to wear them out of good care for ourselves, our children, and one another.

Even during trying times, being treated as though we live in a nanny state only breaks the will of a free people.

How?

Forced control, by design, creates reliance and complacency. We've seen this many times throughout history, including Nazi Germany during WWII, Soviet-supported Cuba, Argentina's Pinochet regime, and Stalin's iron rule of the Soviet Union. Governments can be very good at convincing us that they are keeping us safe or alive. They're very good at telling us if we don't listen to the government, we will all die.

That's crazy. And it's also not true. It's all a con for power.

But that which we believe comes true for us.

A government should affirm its citizens, not treat them like children or, worse, as if they are prisoners. Treating citizens that way says, "You are the problem. You can't be trusted. You must do this and that, and you will owe your life to me."

What a government should say to its citizens is, "We are all in this together, and we exist in a country that rewards innovation. Let's change the world together, as free people always have."

5

FEDERALISM AND THE PANDEMIC

OUR DECLARATION OF INDEPENDENCE SAYS THAT OUR RIGHTS TO BE happy and free come from a power much greater than the government. They are unalienable rights and they were endowed to us by a Creator.

No individual, no government, can take those away because they mean something more than we do.

Our legal system was established during a period of tremendous apprehension over executive authority. We had just emerged from the control of an oppressive king. It was important to the founders to state that the privilege of living doesn't come from our governors or the president of the United States. I live or die because of the choices I make. I am a free person or am not free person because of the choices I make. I don't need my state's governor or anybody else to make those decisions for me. And, I won't let them. I'll die a free person before I live under the tyranny of anybody else telling me that I need to do something because their interests are theirs and not mine.

When there is no nanny to take care of us, we must take care of ourselves. Think about the way certain neighborhoods take care of themselves and one another. That's who we are as Americans. We are not a community of cowards sent to our rooms to hide under our bed until the big bad wolf goes away. Forcing people to go through something with blind faith and no control over setting their course is about collecting and retaining power and control. It's about ruling people.

We don't do that as Americans. It's not who we are.

If there is one prevailing principle in the Constitution, it is to avoid the concentration of power, and the Constitution does so in myriad ways. The Tenth Amendment was written to help ensure that the federal government would not be able to impose the kind of absolute authority the framers feared. The Tenth Amendment says, "The powers not delegated to the United States by the Constitution, nor prohibited by it to the States, are reserved to the States respectively, or to the people." One of those powers, "police powers," was therefore reserved to the states as a power not delegated to the United States. States were granted the power to establish and enforce laws protecting the welfare, safety, and health of the public. This was adopted by early colonial America from English Common Law principles limiting private rights when necessary as a way of safeguarding the common good.

The idea of federalism, in which individual states were granted a large degree of autonomy rather than the centralized state, was one of the ways the framers sought to avoid authoritarianism. The other was to limit the possibility of what's known as a "constitutional drift," a way in which members or branches of the federal government might slowly expand their authority. This drift was prevented by creating limitations on the powers of the federal government. Any and all of those things are vested in the power of the people of those states. A federal government that had power over the people and was more powerful than the individual state governments was seen as dangerous because it would take the power away from the people, putting it further out of reach and making it harder for people to change laws.

It's much easier to get your local government to do something than your state legislature, just as it is easier to get your state to make changes than it is to get Congress to do something. Think of the Tenth Amendment as a consolidation of power to the people or, better yet, a way to make sure the decisions that really matter in the daily lives of Americans are made by the people.

The founders were prolific writers. James Madison and Alexander Hamilton were far from inarticulate or unintentional people. They certainly could have written the document differently, but they said everything they intended. They argued, fought, disagreed, and compromised over every word. These rights were not meant to be fluid, situational, or circumstantial. They just are.

To have a clearer picture of the Tenth Amendment, it must be read together with the Fourteenth Amendment. The Tenth Amendment says, "The powers not delegated to the United States by the Constitution, nor prohibited by it to the States, are reserved to the States respectively, or to the people"—in other words, that everything in these last nine amendments is the responsibility of the federal government, but everything else is the responsibility of the states.

No one can violate any of these federally protected liberties, because a right to freedom of speech guaranteed by the First Amendment might matter in something that the state might be regulating under a Tenth Amendment issue. That's the importance of the Fourteenth Amendment's connection to the Tenth Amendment. While the Tenth Amendment expands the power of the state governments, the Fourteenth Amendment ties all of those other rights back together and says each state still has to respect all of the federally protected rights. Without a robust Fourteenth Amendment standard, we would be left with states that could radically abridge the civil rights of their citizens.

Whenever we have a national tragedy, whether it was something like 9/11, the COVID-19 pandemic, or even the anthrax attacks, there's always a struggle to understand the role of federal versus state involvement. The anthrax letters were a US Postal Service crime, so there was no doubt that the federal government would have absolute authority and jurisdiction in that regard. We have to be able to respond to situations that entice liberty restrictions in a different way. The Constitution requires us to look at these types of situations, not from the lens of, "What can we do to make us safe?" but, "Whatever we do, we must protect those sacrosanct rights."

After 9/11, George Bush rallied to open air travel as quickly as we safely were able. He didn't want people believing the world had changed forever. I challenge you that no one alive now thinks the world hasn't changed as a result of the attacks, but at the time, George Bush understood the importance of restoring American confidence and the belief that we could return to the way things had always been and overcome.

We've lost that. And we didn't lose it because we needed to. We didn't lose it because forty cities had hospitals that were overflowing. We lost it because the government said, "Take a knee on this one." It's as if they didn't want American exceptionalism. It's as if they needed American cowardice. Understand, if they provoked cowardice from us, they could control us. The elites who control government forced us to take a knee and then they put their knee in our backs. Those people are determined to be and stay in control when this is all over. But remember, it is American exceptionalism that is loosening their power grab. It is what is making rising groups like Antifa and the extreme nationalist groups have open combat in the streets of American cities. Everything is bubbling up and the form and function of control here is about making sure that "they," the elites of our country, don't lose power in a scary and rapidly changing situation.

Federalism was not designed to combat an infection; it was designed to combat autocracy. The principles of federalism would require the state to be primarily responsible to prepare for and to deal with pandemics such as the COVID-19 virus When COVID-19 hit the United States, it certainly wasn't the first time our country faced a national quarantine. We saw it during the 1918 Spanish flu, and other times throughout our history. This time, though, something was different. Our leadership was completely unprepared, and the president played down the severity of the virus until it was too late.

During the recent pandemic, people flocked to science for answers. Science is important. Liberty is critical. Science is information. Liberty is power. We should use science to make decisions as free people, not to destroy free America in the process. Likewise, when we allow the government to take full power, inevitable abuses occur.

When President Trump stated that, "when somebody is president of the United States, his authority is total," he was wrong. The Constitution was written precisely to deny that type of claim. *This* is not debatable. A president doesn't get constitutional authority simply by claiming it. What he tried to do and what he was authorized by the Constitution to do were two different things.

At one point early in the pandemic, when asked about governors' complaints that the federal government was not doing enough to help them, President Trump denied that it was his responsibility to supply the states with the medicine and equipment needed to contain and treat the virus. And when pressured to issue a nationwide stay-at-home order, Trump said he preferred to leave it up to each governor to impose such restrictions. Then, in one of his more questionable statements, he claimed that the governors had been able to impose these orders only because he allowed them to do it. He claimed he could have declared a national quarantine earlier, which contradicted his previous statements. Even more important, that contradicted what the Constitution states.

This is why individual-liberty determinations are most important in the United States. If your individual liberty matters as much as mine and we're the arbiter of protecting it, then it's up to us to take care of one another. That was the foundation on which our government was based.

The way free people survive is to unite and assert individual liberty so we can take our country back. But the elites don't survive that way. Elites can only survive if the backs of the free people are broken. No matter how bad it gets, they will be in control and will always be able to pick up the pieces. Meanwhile, everyone else is left for dead, starving, homeless, and out of work.

In a post-COVID-19 environment, many people assume we will be in a recession and possibly headed for a depression. Positive economic growth results after the country initially reopened were largely based on fake money, "stimulus money" pumped into the economy by the government. However, that money will eventually run out. And then what?

Some people believe it's going to be very bad while others think it will be less so. Some people imagine we are going to end up on bread lines while others think we are going to end up with people dying of hunger in the streets.

Some imagine we are headed for a civil war.

When our backs are against the wall, human nature is motivated to do the thing that isn't necessarily in the best interest of the people. Survival instincts say to do what's in your best interest first. In a crisis, if you are the elite, you want to be the person in power when all is said and done. But you can't be that person if your

6

THE UNITED STATES OF HYPOCRISY

"WE WERE WRONG FOR NOT LISTENING TO NFL PLAYERS EARLIER."

This is how NFL Commissioner Roger Goodell began his apology to players who were protesting police brutality in the four years leading up to his mea culpa. Controversy has plagued the NFL since it refused to support Colin Kaepernick and other players who knelt in protest. President Trump encouraged team owners to fire players who protested, even going so far as to say they were ruining the game. While Goodell called President Trump's comments "divisive," he still refused to support protesting players.

It took three years and the deaths of George Floyd, Ahmaud Arbery, and Breonna Taylor to bring centuries of silence, inequality, and oppression of blacks in America by the police state to light and for the NFL to admit that their refusal to listen to and understand their players earlier was a mistake. The NFL decided not to hear their players. Some team owners went so far as to banish their players from kneeling during the playing of the national anthem. Teams are private companies, and they certainly had that choice. Turns out, they were wrong, and now, in 2020, they are paying for it. Who would have guessed they would be wrong? Anyone who believes in individual liberty, even for people with whom you disagree.

Film director and activist Spike Lee thought Goodell's apology was, "weak, it was piss-poor and plain bogus." He didn't understand how Goodell could apologize for the NFL's "misguided acts" without even mentioning Kaepernick. NFL Hall of Famer Terrell Owens led a protest calling on Goodell to personally apologize to Colin Kaepernick for how the league reacted and to their resistance to permitting teams to engage him. And several black NFL players called upon the league to admit officials were wrong for silencing players who peacefully protested and to condemn racism. They made a video together where they each stated, "I am George Floyd."

Two months later, Philadelphia Eagles player DeSean Jackson posted several anti-Semitic posts on Instagram. There was no mass outrage from the NFL and no immediate reaction or punishment from his team. They eventually described his posts as "offensive" and "appalling" and took nearly a week to figure out how to respond. They fined him an undisclosed amount of money. Some other players even came to his defense. As of the writing of this book, Goodell had no league reaction.

How do you separate one hate from all hate? You can't.

The reason Nexus Derechos Humanos Law (NDH), the law firm we fund, files the types of cases we do is simple: I have a vendetta against hypocrisy. When hypocrisy affects me or someone I love or respect, it becomes a fight. The fight isn't personally against any person or group. It's against hypocrisy itself.

NDH has been involved for more than a year in a case in Alabama where a police officer shot and killed an unarmed black teenager. Our law firm represents his estate in a lawsuit against the police who were involved in the killing. The police department's version of the story is that the teen was armed. However, through discovery we learned that, despite the shooter's claim that the teen had a gun, there were at least ten other officers present on the scene, none of whom reported ever seeing a gun on the young man. In our lawsuit, we maintain that they planted a weapon on the dead body of the teenager after he had been transported to the local emergency room. After the body arrived, they asked the doctors and nurses to clear the room so they could conduct their "search." Once the room was empty, they placed a gun inside the basketball shorts of the teen. It was only later in the investigation that we were able to garner a confession from one of the officers, whereby he admitted the gun wasn't in our client's possession. This appears to be a situation where the police created a new narrative, one which made them the victims of this innocent young man.

Sadly, this happens every day.

To me, this case is just one example of the kind of hypocrisy on display from federal, state, and local governments because they believe they have the absolute right to control all people, even if it means setting them up for a crime they didn't commit. Unless you believe the interests of the majority are more important than the interests of freedom, governments simply don't wield that control.

The work we fund is important to setting critical and necessary legal precedence, but we aren't exactly the ACLU. Founded in 1917, the National Civil Liberties Bureau, as it was known then, was created, in part, to oppose the draft and protect conscientious objectors to World War I. At the time, they were subject to restrictions on what they could say for their choice to avoid service. It was originally a committee within the American Union Against Militarism, but it separated due to conflicted viewpoints on governments war policies. The group was reorganized as the American Civil Liberties Union in 1920. When the NCLB first launched, *The New York Times* ran an editorial called, "Jails Are Waiting for Them," which stated that, "sensible people of good will do not make the mistake of believing that speech can be literally and completely free in any civilized country."[6] The article went on to say, "Inevitably there must be restrictions on speech." The editorial took direct aim at the work the NCLB was doing but slammed it as, "antagonizing the settled policies of our Government, of resisting the execution of its deliberately formed plans, and of gaining for themselves immunity from the application of laws to which good citizens willingly submit as essential to the national existence and welfare."

Even President Woodrow Wilson had his concerns. Wilson believed that free speech didn't always apply during wartime, arguing for a censorship provision in the Espionage Act of 1917. He felt censorship was necessary to public safety. His provisions were not passed, but that didn't stop the government from suppressing the activities of the National Civil Liberties Bureau.

Today, the ACLU picks battles they feel they can win and battles they feel have the maximum opportunity for success. When you are that selective in the cases you take on, it's easy to build an incredible looking organization, but you don't help a lot of people. Due to its nature as a non-profit organization, they cannot take all cases that come their way. In fact, they can only take a select few. When they do, they have to rely on other firms offering pro bono representation like we do. Therefore, the number of people who go to the ACLU for help and then actually receive help is surprisingly low.

When we created Nexus Derechos Humanos Law, we set out to do things a little differently than the ACLU. To start, I knew we needed the right leader for the firm. I can fund a law firm, but I can't own one because I am not a licensed attorney. I can't control a law firm any more than a client can control their lawyer (and, if you've ever hired a lawyer, you know that can be challenging). I was blessed to meet Mario Williams, a man whom I knew immediately upon meeting shared the same vision as me. I partnered with Mario, who is now the President of Nexus Derechos Humanos.

Mario is a young African-American man from the South. He worked tirelessly to attend a boutique law school in the Pacific Northwest. His experiences there, and his work abroad in the Peace Corps, gave him a similar view on liberty and civil rights that my jail experience had given me. Since I can't control a law firm, I have to trust the lawyer who leads it. I do that by donating millions of dollars year over year to keep the firm operational. I simply couldn't advance these issues without Mario and his team. The firm was established as a regular law firm, one that we founded to support our clients and the people we serve. In our world, everyone who calls us gets heard. We don't just take cases we know we can win. For us, the cases we aren't sure of are the ones that accomplish something for the people and their liberty interest. That's our mission statement. It would be the height of hypocrisy to say we believe in civil liberties but we are only going to fight for it when we think we can win.

We never think we can separate ourselves enough from the cause without getting dirty. Here's what I mean: The ACLU fought for the right of the Unite the Right Rally in Charlottesville and then abdicated that fight after the riots. They were correct to protect the right of the Unite the Right to have the rally. They had a right to be there, and so did the protesters. Like the local authorities, the ACLU stepped away from that fight after taking serious heat regarding the racist views and actions of the person they were representing. Richard Spencer, the leader of the Unite the Right rally, initially asked us to defend and help him in his effort to sue the City of Charlottesville.

I immediately called Mario to see how he would feel. There's no question Richard Spencer is a racist, so I knew making the call to Mario was a big ask. Of course, he was offended by the idea, but he also understood that even if we don't like what Spencer and his group stands for, they had the right to hold their rally. I understood that Mario was not willing to represent Spencer in a prospective lawsuit against Charlottesville, so I began to consider whether another attorney we work with might be interested in the case. I agreed with Mario that Spencer has despicable views. That being true, I truly believe that every human being in Charlottesville deserved a police force that wouldn't effectively incite a race riot by bringing two enraged groups together and then standing down. I believe in constitutional principles of liberty, which means we must fight for them even when we don't subscribe to the message.

I found an attorney who was willing to consider taking the case. Our condition was simple: as long as Spencer agreed to give any proceeds to the anti-defamation league and the NAACP, we would agree to give our time. Spencer rejected the offer. And, thank God he said no. We would have done it because it was the right thing to do, but it would have been a tough pill to swallow.

That's what *not* being hypocritical looks like. In a hypocritical America, doing the right thing somehow looks weird. And being hypocritical has somehow become the norm.

As president of the United States, Donald Trump had a significant pattern of self-contradiction, often thinking something is okay when he does it or if it benefits him but not okay when others do the same thing. I am not sure that President Trump is truly a hypocrite, but he is who he is.

Maya Angelou once said, "When people show you who they are, believe them." Before the election in 2016, according to Trump, the Electoral College was a "disaster." After the election, he called it "genius." He is completely comfortable with "alternative facts," yet he despises the media and calls it "fake news." He is not the first president to suffer from hyperactive hypocrisy. There were many moments in the presidencies of Obama and Clinton that easily rivaled Trump's hypocrisy. But Trump certainly kept hypocrisy in the forefront of just about everything involving his presidency, especially when members of his cabinet were "winners" when they started and "losers" when their service ended. Even distinguished generals took scathing public blows from the president.

Yet barely five minutes went by without a pro-Trump conservative accusing a liberal of hypocrisy for criticizing the president's misleading statements and outright lies. Republicans often find themselves in an awkward position. Hurling allegations of hypocrisy at the president's critics was a convenient way of protecting Trump while looking for ways to weaken the effectiveness of those making the allegations. Defenders said things like, "You say Trump lies, but what about when Obama said everyone would be able to keep their health insurance under the Affordable Care Act?" Or they brought up the Clintons, whether it was the Benghazi attack, Hillary's emails, or even the treatment of Monica Lewinsky. Politics—even modern, deflationary, liberal politics—is a domain of life structured around appeals to higher standards. To be fair, there are many things about Trump and his presidency that I really appreciate. I have to start with criminal-justice reform. The man has done more as president on this issue than any in modern history. Unfortunately, that isn't saying much, but it's a start, perhaps a short-lived one given the president's move away from criminal justice reform and toward "total domination." In July 2020, Axios reported: "President Trump has told people in recent days that he regrets following some of son-in-law and senior adviser Jared Kushner's political advice—including supporting criminal justice reform—and will stick closer to his own instincts…"[7]

Additionally, before the coronavirus pandemic, his economic policies were providing job growth and stability for industry in America, especially for small businesses. I expected Trump might do well with the economy when he was elected, and he exceeded my expectations in that regard before the pandemic.

His appointment of Neil Gorsuch to the Supreme Court was a real win, to use his vernacular, for the American people. I didn't think so at first, but as I read his extensive body of legal opinions before his appointment, I began to realize that he was a different kind of judge. He is a fierce believer in individual liberty. While he is nowhere near perfect, his presence on the Supreme Court gives me hope that we might just survive all these uncharted waters and find our better selves again someday.

However, as a pastor and a man of deep principled faith in the teachings of Jesus of Nazareth, I find Trump's patterns of womanizing, hypocrisy, and misogyny unacceptable. Although he identifies as being a Republican, when you get right down to it, he is the ultimate white liberal. White liberalism is a belief where a person with seemingly progressive ideology believes they are needed by minorities to accomplish equal opportunity. They pander when they feel like it or they ignore the realities of the policies they support because they just don't care. It's the ultimate ends justifying the means. For Trump, he'll pay lip service to the black community in front of Kim Kardashian and Kanye West, but then he will act in heinous ways when he doesn't have to look them in the face. He is not afraid to blow the race whistle if he thinks it's going to get him votes or make money.

Why can he get away with this? Because he doesn't care if the ends justify the means. From a faith perspective, President Trump is like the ultimate Hollywood liberal, with much more in common with Jeffrey Epstein and Harvey Weinstein than with Ralph Reed or Pat Robertson.

The United States of Hypocrisy is brought into even clearer focus when you consider that perhaps the most immoral, unethical, hypocritical tyrant to ever take the office of president would receive the blessing and absolute advocacy from the religious right, which is predominantly made up of Christian activists. Note the word *Christ* in "Christian." That alone is revolting to any pastor or person who believes in the personal relationship with God that Jesus taught. Any person put on this earth who believes their purpose is to teach people how to have such a relationship would be horrified at the idea that any of the resources of a church named after Jesus of Nazareth would be used to support such a person who isn't just broken, but who lives, thrives, and relishes in that brokenness. That isn't of God. That's just evil.

Understand what I am saying and what I am not saying. If you believe you should support someone like Donald Trump despite his sins because you believe he is the best candidate, then you should vote your conscience. But I believe we should not worship any candidate or make idols out of politicians or the presidency.

Sadly, we have tyranny in the temple of democracy right now, and in the temple of democracy, Jesus would have overturned tyranny. If I want to be authentic, then I can't support tyranny and freedom at the same time. If I did, I'd be no better than any hypocrite in Washington. I believe that freedom comes from God, and, therefore, it cannot be taken away—certainly not by our government leaders. They are not God. I reject anyone who believes they have the power to take away my freedoms. I am sure there are those of you reading this who might not agree with this stance. Handing over rights that God gave us to any human being, at least without due process of law, just feels wrong to me. And I am not prepared to do that. Not for a president or anyone who believes they wield more power over the people than the people have over their government. Now, maybe, just maybe, there are some people who are willing to do that—who have done that—but there is a price to pay.

And that price might just be the heart and soul of our Republic.

Unfortunately, both sides are guilty of deploying double standards, hypocritically claiming to take a stand on the basis of an elevated principle. And both sides engage in flagrant partisanship, attacking a political opponent for something that would never set off alarms if it were said or done by a political ally. Is it politically effective? In some cases, perhaps. But it's undeniably bad for the civic culture of the United States.

You can fight if you have rules. Remember, we once had a vice president of the United States of America shoot and kill a man. When Aaron Burr shot Alexander Hamilton, there were rules. It was a duel, where the terms were structured before they took aim at each other, based on an idea of individual liberty—the biggest one. At the time, this is how certain conflicts were resolved. It isn't something we should want for our future, but it is part of our past. The lessons were passed on, even if duels were not. In the days of dueling, problems got resolved. Today, partisan problems, by nature, are problems never meant to be resolved. They are merely for politicians to raise money and manipulate voters.

But when we engage in partisan politics, we lose the structure of the Constitution. We lose the structure of our liberty interests. And when conservatives approve of the president of the United States using armed federal troops to attack peaceful protestors, those conservatives abdicate credibility and lose the moral high ground needed to defend the Constitution and any rights we may be losing, including the rights guaranteed by the Second Amendment.

Hypocrisy is the enemy of liberty.

I am not suggesting we go back to the days of duels. Americans have to structure our government around a principle of individual liberty. The willingness to accept what is unacceptable just to get a political advantage means that everything you believe in as principle is gone.

I have wept with my conservative and militia friends who speak passionately about what happened at Ruby Ridge to Randy Weaver and his family after some of them were slaughtered by government agents. But if those I commiserated with support the president attacking peaceful protestors, they are part of the problem of hypocrisy.

We can all lose our way. The guiding light must be our Constitution. That's literally the point of that document. It is a beacon of hope and promise, if only we would pay attention to it. I am sure many of you find yourself living in the gray these days. Things aren't quite black or white. The labels that we once proudly wore no longer seem to fit. You may be searching for something or someone you can look toward for the future. It's an easy answer. The Constitution can be that anchor. You can love and support whomever you want so long as what he or she does is consistent with that document. And when what they do is inconsistent with the Constitution, you have no choice but to speak up and call them out. If you don't, then the document doesn't mean anything anymore.

If nothing else, one thing I know that unites all of us is our disdain for the "do as I say, not as I do" methodology we endure from our political leaders in this country, whether it's on a federal, state, or local level. We had governors like Virginia's Northam implementing executive orders requiring us to wear masks and socially distance ourselves, yet they go out in public without a mask, greet people, and take pictures beside them. In Virginia, if your business doesn't require your customers to wear masks, the state can revoke your business license.

Governor Gretchen Whitmer of Michigan shut down all of the marinas in her state when she ordered Michigan's initial shut-down order. As Memorial Day weekend approached, the governor loosened restrictions and specifically asked people not to flock to the state's waterfront areas so that the viral spread could be contained. However, at the same time, the governor's husband was calling to have his boat placed in the water, and he wanted it done in front of others who were waiting. When he was told that it would not be possible to accommodate him, he reportedly asked the marina owner if his status as the governor's husband would get him in front of the line. When called out, the governor's husband said he was just joking.

Which is it, Governor? Is the pandemic serious enough for you to take away the civil rights of Michiganders, but worthy of jokes from your husband about using your office to get some special favors?

The people in Michigan, especially on the right, were justifiably angry over the obscene hypocrisy from the leader of their state and her husband. The militia folks were affected by Governor Whitmer's hypocrisy, too, and they protested to show how they felt about it.

New Mexico Governor Michelle Lujan Grisham shut down all the retail stores and then called her personal jeweler and placed an order for jewelry—in the middle of the pandemic!

If this sounds like a vendetta to you, that's because it is! It's a vendetta against hypocrisy. I have no tolerance for those who use hypocrisy to manipulate people to further their own interests. Where is the personal responsibility?

As demoralizing as it is to be reminded of the hypocrisy of those leading and serving our country, our very revulsion at their vices is a powerful tribute to just how strongly we remain attached to standards of virtue. And when we've had enough, we stand up for what we truly believe in. That is the power of America and her people.

By design or by default, what many hadn't seen until recently is the grotesque hypocrisy of the police state. When something doesn't affect people, they tend not to notice what is happening in the "other" neighborhoods where they are heavily policed. And to be certain, its exactly that kind of hypocrisy that black and brown Americans have understood for a really long time. How are they supposed to get along with a police structure that our government tells them to support when they watch those very same officers kill their brothers and sisters and then get a paid vacation afterward?

Cops who kill are always treated differently. But wouldn't we want the same healthy investigation, no matter who was suspected of killing someone? Who wouldn't want a healthy and robust investigation when a police officer kills another human being? Could it be the police state? Police unions? America will not be free so long as a young black kid who is suspected of homicide goes to jail, but a white police officer suspected of the same offense gets vacation, desk duty, and all the benefit of the doubt he can handle.

Such is reality in The United States of Hypocrisy.

that number. And yet, our government constantly tells us we need to double down and spend more.

The criminal-justice system doesn't work and doubling down and spending more on it won't change the outcome.

When we oppress people, they eventually fight back. And when they do, we are left with total distrust, fear, and a permanent underclass in society. It's simply not American to deprive people of individual liberty while we lead the world in incarceration per capita, higher than any other government in the world. Let me be clear here: The United States represents about 4 percent of the world's population, yet the United States prison population represents 22 percent of the world's prisoners. In 2017, we spent $79 billion on imprisoning people in the United States.

We are not a free America.

In our efforts to fight this injustice, the work we fund creates a lot of problems for very powerful and wealthy government elites. The result is that I command a company that has been under constant investigation for seven years. Here's a list of the entities who have investigated us for our unapologetic service to God's flock:

- Washington State Attorney General
- Massachusetts Attorney General (ongoing)
- New York Attorney General
- Virginia Attorney General
- California Division of Insurance
- United States Department of Labor
- Homeland Security Investigations
- ICE
- Sarah Saldana, Director of ICE Inquiry
- Congressional investigation request by California Congresswoman Norma Torres
- Senate Homeland Security Committee
- Class-action counsel
- Augusta County (Virginia) Sheriff Donald Smith
- Fairfax County (Virginia) Police

- Fairfax City (Virginia) Police
- The Government of Guatemala

Seven years later, most of those investigations are long closed with no action, only to be replaced with new ones. Strangely, they seem to come from areas where we've "stuck our nose" in the business of government elites.

In 2015, I moved my company's corporate campus to rural western Virginia, in Augusta County. Our company's focus on serving immigrants and criminal defendants can make us unpopular in small rural communities who do not initially understand the benefit of the work we do. Add to that mix my felony convictions for check-related charges in my youth, and we become an easy target for investigations and government attacks.

Sometimes, even I can be surprised by the extent to which these attacks on our civil liberties will go. This is certainly the case in Augusta County.

In 2016, I found evidence that Donald Smith, the newly elected sheriff of Augusta County, Virginia, his command staff, local bail bondsmen, and the local prosecutor banded together to attempt to end my business. How did I find out? The answer underscores just how not free we all are right now.

If you are a convicted felon, it's very difficult to rent an apartment or home. Most housing developments have policies against renting to felons. We didn't think this was right, as we believe everyone deserves a second, third, or fourth chance in life. "Homes by Nexus" is a subsidiary of our parent company, Nexus Services, which helps provide rental housing to people who can't qualify because of prior criminal histories. The builder we use for development is called Countryside Homecrafters. The CEO of Countryside, a gregarious man named Frank Root with a larger-than-life personality, is the kind of person who has significant clout in his community, earned through being trustworthy, consistent, and reliable.

After we contracted with his company, Frank shared that he had previously filed suit against Augusta County after his permits for a development were denied. He had found that in their hostility to his housing projects and attempts to stop him, local officials had acted unlawfully. He litigated all the way to the Supreme Court of Virginia, where Frank prevailed.

Intrigued, I decided to read that case and began to see patterns of similarities between that case and the unusual delays that were happening to us. In Frank's case, the county likely plotted against his business because he is a developer. Local politicians have love/hate relationships with developers. In our case, I wondered, *Were they angry about the houses we were building or our campus expansion?* I needed to know.

I felt our efforts to support disadvantaged people with pro bono counsel likely had something to do with their behavior.

We submitted a Freedom of Information Act (FOIA) request to the county asking for any emails containing the names of our executive team and our companies. FOIA is an incredibly powerful tool that often exposes government corruption. At the time, we were experiencing delays in building dozens of houses and offices in the county, and I hoped a FOIA might give us a small glimpse into the rationale behind the delays. We sent a letter to the county's IT department citing the FOIA law and simply asked for any email mentioning all of our executive or company names. Several days later we got our answer.

What we discovered was nothing short of shocking.

First, it's important to recall that the name of my company is Nexus Services, Inc. The reason that matters is that "Nexus" is a legal term of art. It can be found when describing the connection between any two things in an investigation, for example drugs and guns. That is in no way why I named the company Nexus of course, but this fact is relevant to this story that follows.

Several days after filing the FOIA request, we heard from the county attorney that we could pick up a jump drive with a few hundred responsive results. I was surprised that there would be hundreds of emails, and I was quite certain that I was about to get some intel into what the county was doing and whether they had violated my rights.

I had no idea what I was about to discover.

The jump drive did not contain a few hundred responses. It contained nearly 10,000. Several thousand were emails between law-enforcement agents at the state and federal level that contained the word "nexus" but had nothing to do with us. However, thousands of them absolutely were about me and my company.

And some of them made clear the hostility that we faced. A local bail-bond agent went out of his way to create a narrative that was based on what was good for him and his business. He clearly had the ear of the sheriff's department. A local bail-bond agent copies the sheriff on his theories and creates an ongoing investigation into my companies because he was afraid? It's absurd.

As I would discover in one of those conspiratorial emails, the local bail agent summed it up best: In complaining about my company's charitable bail-bonding program, the largest in the country, the bail agent pleaded for help from a detective who used to work for him, as well as from the sheriff and the prosecutor. He clearly wanted us gone because, as he wrote, "None of us can compete with free."

The emails I discovered from the FOIA request made clear that we were the target of a number of investigations seeking to show that we were involved in illegal activities. We uncovered not-yet-executed plans to raid our offices, as well as the existence of a detective who had been attempting to build a network of CIs (confidential informants) to provide him evidence that I was committing some kind of criminal activity. They had even enlisted one of our managers as a confidential informant. While he was successful in enlisting the aid of one of our managers, they were unable to find any evidence of wrongdoing, and their disappointment seemed clear.

With every failed attempt to take us down, their emails became more frustrated and bitter. They were unhappy that we were a legitimate business providing important services. At one point, the prosecutor exclaimed through a county email server, "I really can't stand these people." I was sure that the sheriff was more than willing to commit his law-enforcement resources to try to generate a bogus case where none existed.

For the better part of a year, this scheme ran without our knowledge. But with this FOIA response in hand, we were now armed with the most powerful thing you can ever have when you're under attack by a corrupt government: *knowledge.*

In an effort to offer an olive branch and clear up any misunderstanding the local sheriff had, I offered to come to his office and open my books for him. For his part, he denied that this witch hunt existed, despite his being copied on, and responding to, emails seeking to find some alleged crime with which to charge me or my employees. This futile investigation was confusing and maddening, especially as the investigations continued, which I began to feel were turning spiteful. I experiences a number of incidents that appeared to demonstrate that my family and I were being inexplicably targeted. These included everything from petty acts of harassment to my vehicle being run off the interstate with my child in the car and attempts to plant drugs on me.

We became convinced that our business was under attack, as we were personally, and decided that we had to bring another lawsuit against the authorities, this time on our own behalf.

The judge in the case, Elizabeth K. Dillon of the Western District of Virginia, formerly served as an attorney for local governments defending cases such as these. Judge Dillon is a brilliant jurist, but she shows a pattern of ruling for the government in lawsuits against them. From the start, I felt the judge hated this lawsuit.

We were soon embroiled in expensive and time-consuming litigation on a case where the court was clearly hostile toward our position. It was costing hundreds of thousands of dollars a month. After assessing, I decided that money could be spent on funding more lawsuits on behalf of people who aren't able to defend themselves. So we decided to drop our lawsuit. To add to my frustration, after we dropped the suit, we were then ordered to pay part of the defendants' legal fees. The judge felt we had not litigated in good faith. I believe that while the judge no doubt believes her ruling, she found it difficult to acknowledge wrongdoing by government authorities. I believe Judge Dillon truly thought our litigation was filed in bad faith, but it wasn't. We filed the lawsuit because we were convinced the local government was wrongfully threatening our business and our personal safety. And I believe the court's hostility to the case indicates people, especially in this part of Virginia, really can't sue the government, whether it's local, state, or federal, and my heart broke for the scores of people whose rights have been violated.

What we face in our community feels oddly personal and vicious, but it does nopthing to change our mission to serve the people churned through the system each and every day. I have no problem with the government or the police, but I have a huge problem with hypocrisy and wrongdoing.

When we find it, we go after it—hard.

Another example of our dedication to eradicating hypocrisy and corruption involves a lawsuit we filed in New York against Central American Legal Assistance (CALA), a legal-aid group, for cutting off Libre by Nexus-provided ankle bracelets that our immigrant clients were wearing. The group thought the bracelets our company provided were simply an effort to earn recurring revenue. While we did charge a monthly fee, they failed to consider the life-sustaining services we provide, such as release from custody, access to free legal services, access to free medical services, and access to transportation services. For our clients, the fee is nominal for the services they receive, and most are incredibly grateful.

While the mission of CALA and Nexus is similar, especially around most immigration issues, their firm behaved as criminals when they destroyed the ankle bracelets, which are our private property. We settled the suit to our satisfaction and continued serving New York clients. So I was surprised when we received a subpoena from Eric Schneiderman, the then New York attorney general about an investigation into our company just a few months after the CALA suit concluded. I did not think the investigation was a coincidence.

The New York attorney general wanted all of our client records. We then received similar missives from the attorneys general in Washington State, Massachusetts, and Virginia. Those were followed by investigations from divisions of insurance in Virginia, New York, Washington State, and California. A week later we received the same request from the Consumer Financial Protection Bureau (CFPB), a behemoth of a federal agency that is supposed to regulate lenders.

Lenders—why were they investigating Nexus?

My head was spinning. The whole matter seemed clearly to be an attempt to shut down our company. And if it had been any other company, it likely would have worked.

Despite funding several law firms, we were forced to hire outside counsel who specialized in defending government investigations. How was I going to afford the millions of dollars in legal fees I knew it would cost to respond and defend these requests?

Even more important to me than the money involved, how could I, in good conscience, turn over this information to offices that might share it with ICE?

What duty did I owe our clients to protect their privacy? These were just some of the questions rushing through my mind as I prepared to go into battle protecting God's flock.

I responded by filing a lawsuit against both the New York attorney general and the Virginia attorney general. I similarly filed suit against the CFPB, challenging the CFPB's authority to investigate our companies since we aren't lenders of money. When it came to the attorneys general, my request was simple: Enter a confidentiality order protecting our clients, and I will give you anything you want. Don't agree, and you won't get anything.

That attitude, I soon learned, was not appreciated by the various attorneys general offices. The result was protracted litigation, in which I argued for client protections and they argued I couldn't set the terms of their investigations.

Think about that for a second: They are investigating me. They sent me a subpoena. That process demands a response. The only response the government was willing to listen to was capitulation without argument. That isn't what I provided.

See where this is going?

I wouldn't forget my promise to God to serve His flock, and I will never abandon our clients. While we were fighting in courts in New York and Virginia, the attorneys general in Massachusetts and Washington State agreed to our requested protections. Massachusetts has these protections by statute, but in Washington, Attorney General Bob Ferguson took the time to protect our clients by crafting a confidentiality agreement we could accept, one that actually protected our clients from disclosure of their personal private family information.

This is a right any of us should expect under due process and right to privacy, and it's one I was determined to fight to protect for my clients.

As we continued to fight in court, the attorneys general of Virginia and New York argued that the agreement I sought was unnecessary. They said the disclosures

I feared might happen—intensely personal family information being divulged—would never be disclosed by them because they care about immigrants. But they refused to commit to that in writing, which made me nervous. I remained unrelenting in my pursuit of protection.

So I was then surprised to find out during my litigation that New York and Virginia sued the United States Department of Justice for tethering the receipt of JAG (justice grants) from the DOJ on information sharing related to immigrants. The very fear they claimed in our case would never happen was happening at the exact same time.

I filed a motion to intervene in their case, *New York v. US Department of Justice*.[9]

This didn't go over well.

Our filing suddenly placed us as allies of the very states investigating us, and they hated that. New York asked the court to dispense with our motion immediately without a hearing, but Judge Edgardo Ramos disagreed. A hearing was set for August 21, 2018, and our legal team got to work. The states were openly hostile, which is often a symptom of being caught in your own hypocrisy. After all, these offices just spent hundreds of thousands of taxpayer dollars arguing in court that my request for confidentiality agreements in these inquiries was unnecessary.

I was the last guy they wanted showing up to support my very same argument in a very different case because then they would be forced to admit I was correct.

Judge Ramos listened to our arguments and ruled against our motion to intervene but invited us to file an amicus brief, which is a friend-of-the-court brief, meaning a non-party to a case can give the court advice. With our motion to intervene, we had already filed a factual filing representation of our case supporting the states in their lawsuit against the federal government. So we decided to have the arguments we had already filed stand before the court. We were convinced the judge was going to rule in the states' favor, and we didn't want to slow down the process. Since the judge reasoned that this case was proceeding on an expedited basis and that the issues were fully briefed, we knew he was going to make a quick decision. And he did. Two weeks later he found that our interests could be sufficiently represented by New York in that case. The sting of being exposed as hypocritical was felt hard at the attorney general's office. Judge Ramos ruled in favor of the states against the federal government, a decision that was later overturned on appeal.

Four months later, the New York attorney general filed a motion in the Supreme Court of New York to have me indefinitely jailed for contempt. The contempt was real on both sides, but my contempt was for their hypocrisy and their willingness to abuse their enforcement power to punish those who speak truth to those in power. My contempt started and stopped with an abusive attorney general's office. I have no contempt for any judicial order.

The judge denied their ridiculous request, and I became more focused than ever on fighting to serve the underserved.

I began to truly realize the desperate need for more people to follow the command of Jesus of Nazareth. I realized that God isn't found in what's holy. God is active and available in brokenness—the places where He is most needed.

If we seek brokenness and work to resolve it, we work alongside God. In fact, we are the hands and feet of God on Earth.

I take that responsibility very seriously.

These types of cases affect all of us, but especially those who take on the powerful elite. There are many who do the work of God in very different ways. One such person is my very good friend and television personality Duane "Dog" Chapman, also known as Dog the Bounty Hunter. Dog is America's most iconic bounty hunter, with over 8,000 captures throughout his illustrious career.

Dog and I met over ten years ago in Virginia during a legislative session where we were allies on legislation to protect the Eight Amendment. As a bail bondsman and bounty hunter, Dog knew the bail system inside and out. He was there to testify on behalf of the bail agents. I was a lobbyist representing the bail agents interests as well as criminal defendant interest.

On the surface, you would not expect Dog and me to have much in common. He arrests criminal defendants, while I get them out of jail and often defend them.

However, for each of us, our client's true success almost always comes from a cathartic moment of accountability. The Bible tells us that to everything there is a season, and my universalist faith teaches me that we are part of an interdependent web of existence. We all work together.

With Dog, you can see that in the backseat ministries Dog the Bounty Hunter offers his fugitives after their arrests. The fact is, we have a lot more in common in our beliefs than about that which we disagree.

Consider Dog's most famous capture, that of Max Factor heir Andrew Luster. Luster had been arrested and charged for raping three women, drugging them with the date-rape drug GHB, assaulting them, and videotaping the assaults. Luster posted a one-million-dollar cash bail and was released. When Luster failed to appear in court to defend himself, he was eventually found guilty in absentia of eighty-six counts including rape, sodomy, drug and weapons possession, and poisoning. He was sentenced to 124 years in jail.

Dog and his team believed Luster had fled to Mexico, and he was right. He went to Mexico to capture this privileged fugitive and make things right for the victims. While I defend criminal defendants, the justice only works when victims get their day in court too.

In that sense, Dog and I are on the same mission, doing very different jobs.

After an intense search, Dog apprehended Luster, but they were both arrested. Luster denied it was him, and therefore Dog was accused of kidnapping, a bogus charge that was later reduced to deprivation of liberty by the Mexican federales. Kidnapping is a felony. Deprivation of liberty is a misdemeanor.

Luster was extradited back to America to face his fate, while Dog and his team sat in a Mexican jail for weeks. Eventually, he was released and on the advice of his Mexican legal team, they told him to run—go back to America and never return to Mexico, explaining that he couldn't be extradited on a misdemeanor.

While this advice may sound shocking, it's exactly the advice immigrants receive in America from many immigration attorneys all the time.

Dog and his crew fled, and once they were back on American soil, they were hailed as heroes—that is until the United States government decided to use Dog as a political pawn. Months after his return, Dog awoke to federal marshals wielding guns in his home, arresting him for kidnapping. They were holding a bad warrant consisting of charges that could not be proven and a notice of extradition to Mexico for a crime he did not commit. The government knew it and still allowed this to happen to one of its citizens.

As the Secretary of State at the time, Condoleezza Rice had to personally sign the order, even though twenty-nine members of Congress wrote to her asking her not to. Four years and millions of dollars later, Dog was exonerated, and the government that used him as a political ploy never compensated him. His civic duty was to capture Andrew Luster, a truly evil human being, so his victims could be at peace and know that long-promised justice had been served.

The government threw him to the wolves. From that perspective, we have a lot in common.

To this day, my companies continue to litigate in our hometown to protect the disadvantaged. We continue to be harassed and targeted by the local authorities. As recently as July 2020, my partner, Richard, was arrested on a false charge of perjury after swearing out a protective order when he was assaulted by a stalker pretending to be a process server. Fortunately, we had video evidence from three different sources to prove Richard was, in fact, assaulted, including video from the stalker.

My family and employees live in a state of open hostility with county law enforcement. Richard and I have security 24/7 at our campus and at our home. We've been sued, attacked, investigated, and had our characters assassinated, yet we continue to fight for the meek and weak because that's how we lift up society.

In order to do that, we live in the margins, kind of like Jesus did. And just as He was condemned for his commitment to living in the margins, so is everyone who chooses to serve those whom the government needs to keep as a permanent under-class, people like my partner and me, people like all of our many clients.

Even so, I'm living proof of two things through this: One, the elite government will come after you if you threaten its power. When we began suing governments, we faced investigations and heavy attacks, and because we haven't let up, that hasn't let up. And two, it's a tough road, but you can win because this government is a paper tiger. A sheriff's office in Virginia or the CFPB are very powerful agencies, but our liberty, should it continue to exist, is more powerful. At least it is supposed to be. And that's why those in power want to take it away.

The continued work and success of Nexus shows that if you stand up and fight for your rights, you can protect them. Simply put, when you're right, you fight!

If you go where God sends you, no power on this earth or anywhere else can successfully stand against you. You may not realize the dream in your time here, but your work is part of the larger work of God, and your DNA will be forever emblazoned on advancing humanity, one desperate, meek, and disenfranchised soul at a time. While you're doing the work, you realize how much a part of God's flock you truly are. In moments of true service, human divisions will fall, and the power of that process changes lives.

It's a mission of service worth fighting, living, and dying for.

8

WHEN THE GOVERNMENT TAKES A KNEE

"When civility leads to death, revolting is the only logical reaction. The cries for peace will rain down, and when they do, they will land on deaf ears, because your violence has brought this resistance."
—COLIN KAEPERNICK

IN SEPTEMBER 2016, THERE WAS GREAT ANTICIPATION ABOUT THE SAN Francisco 49ers game against the San Diego Chargers in Qualcomm Stadium. It wasn't one of sports great rivalries that garnered much attention or debate. It was the anticipation that one or perhaps many players from the 49ers would sit out the national anthem. With the first note, San Francisco's quarterback, Colin Kaepernick, knelt to the ground in protest. While some saw his kneeling as a show of disrespect against the flag, his intention was to object respectfully to systemic police brutality against African Americans and other minorities. The fans in Qualcomm stadium booed his decision to take a knee for what he believed in. He was quickly joined by two of his teammates.

In the days that followed, the media created a very divided view of what took place. Some outlets never addressed why Kaepernick knelt in the first place. Instead, their narrative focused on the meaning of the American flag, First Amendment rights, Kaepernick's motivation, and the military.

When Kaepernick took to the field that day, it was his third display of this sort. Until that game in San Diego, his actions had gone relatively unnoticed. Why did this become news? Perhaps it was because he chose to kneel in San Diego, a city where the military is such a prominent presence, or maybe because the people of San Diego feel especially patriotic. Sadly, that game became a singular moment that defined his career.

It also built a movement.

A year later, many professional athletes were "taking a knee" in a show of solidarity. While some people saw protest during the national anthem as disrespectful, militant, angry, or similar to the Black Power salutes raised by Tommie Smith and John Carlos at the 1968 Olympics, the reality is, taking a knee has always been a show of respect and humility. When a black athlete takes a knee during the national anthem, they are not anti-American, they are peacefully protesting police violence against their community, and as an extension of those actions, a criminal-justice system that allows those murders. They are seeking to place a more focused lens on the realities the black and brown communities face in this country. The original act that incited so much emotion has become a gesture of protest.

By sacrificing himself for others, Kaepernick paid the highest price for doing what he believes in: He put his life, career and reputation on the line for other people. How many of us could honestly say we'd rise up or kneel down in the same way?

Kaepernick's taking a knee was reflective of how white America and the elites in privileged America expect "us" to take a knee and to abridge our individual liberty. Kaepernick took a knee in solidarity for black and brown communities. I didn't see it as disrespectful. I saw it as honoring the promise of a not yet realized idea that our amazing flag represents.

Not wanting to pay attention to a problem seems to be an ongoing theme with our government. Instead of calling out tyranny and repression, forces in our government have learned to use their knee in a different way: putting it in our back as a tool of oppression.

Kaepernick's message was simple: "See us." The government's message is the complete opposite: "Don't see what we're doing."

The government does this by creating distractions in an effort to try and convince people that what they are seeing is not really happening or whatever we're seeing is an example of the means justifying the end.

We certainly saw vivid examples during the Charlottesville riots, the early weeks of COVID-19, and after the death of George Floyd. All of America felt the knee in our necks as we collectively mourned the death of Floyd at the hands of four police officers. And like Kaepernick's protest, that, too, has been purposely and methodically propagandized.

This is clear in the strange conflicts occurring across America between left-wing and right-wing activists. The government elite is hard at work fanning the flames of the biases from both groups, while, at times, encouraging open conflict. In reality, the propaganda is designed to keep us from uniting against an out-of-control and un-American government.

I define this "us" as all of us who believe in liberty, all of us who believe in the promise of opportunity America provides, and all of us who haven't yet achieved everything we want.

The natural enemy of this "us" are the elites who have so much. They have forgotten how they achieved their success in the first place and, therefore, prefer to build classes of people who will protect what they own from other people outworking them. It is an affront to the very idea of America.

What happens when we take a knee and the government responds by putting its knee in our backs? Or worse, when the government responds by putting its knee on our necks? That decision to take a knee becomes no longer ours.

It was Kaepernick's decision not to stand for the national anthem. He was in the prime of his career. When he did this, his career was destroyed. And still, that was his choice, a cognitive decision he made to be in that place. That is why I respect his choice so much. He did it knowing it would hurt him, and yet he chose to stand by his convictions. That's as American an attitude as I've ever seen.

I support that in anyone, including people with whom I disagree.

When we are forced to be in that place by our government, their intention is to take away our ability to control what we do. If Kaepernick took a knee to point out how little control everyone has, then the government is forcing us to take a knee to take back our control.

Let's take a look at the event in Charlottesville, Virginia, as an example of our government taking a knee. In August 2017, people gathered in Charlottesville to protest the decision to remove the statue of Confederate General Robert E. Lee from a public park. The rally was organized by Unite the Right member Jason Kessler on August 12, resulting in thousands of people filling the streets the night before.

What happened in Charlottesville should not happen in any modern American city.

Charlottesville is in west-central Virginia, in the foothills of the Blue Ridge Mountains and home of the University of Virginia and its nearly 22,000 college students. It is about one hundred miles southwest of Washington, DC, and only thirty minutes from where I live and work.

The removal of the Robert E. Lee statue was the reason white nationalists and neo-Nazi organizations came to Charlottesville that August. This wasn't the first time there had been protests over the statue's removal. Earlier in 2017, white nationalist Richard Spencer led a rally to protest the removal. Two months later, the Ku Klux Klan rallied in Charlottesville over the plan to remove the statue and rename the park where it sits. The park, now known as Market Street Park, was previously known as Emancipation Park from June 2017 to July 2018 and was originally named Lee Park, in honor of Robert E. Lee. During that rally, Klan members clashed with counterprotestors and the police arrested twenty-three people.

By August 11, rumors began that the Unite the Right rally would have a surprise early start on Friday night. Those rumors proved true when around 8:45 p.m., approximately 250 men dressed in khakis and carrying Tiki torches reminiscent of those carried by lynch mobs in the American South began to gather in an area behind UVA's Memorial Gymnasium called Nameless Field. The men were arranged in formation, two by two. Organizers instructed the group to head to the university's rotunda, where a statue of Thomas Jefferson stands. As they moved across campus, they began to chant, "blood and soil," a Nazi slogan meant to emphasize the racial purity of the people of German blood and their connection to a German homeland, and, "Jews will not replace us." By 9:00 p.m. the group was making its way up the lawn to the Jefferson statue. It was there that they ran into resistance, when about thirty UVA students met them at the base of the statue. The group had locked arms and stood in a circle around the statue at its base. The 250 marchers encircled the students and began shouting, "White Lives Matter!" while making monkey sounds. Within moments, both sides were pushing one another. Soon thereafter, punches were being thrown and torches were being tossed to the ground.

It took university police several minutes to arrive on the scene. When they did, there were people injured on both sides. The clash that Friday night was merely a precursor of things to come the following day.

The rally was set from noon to 5:00 p.m. and was to take place in downtown Charlottesville at Emancipation Park. By 8:00 a.m., the park began to fill. Some people were holding white nationalist banners and Nazi flags, many were carrying sticks, and some were carrying handguns or rifles. Virginia is an open-carry state, which means you can openly carry a firearm in public where it can be seen by others. Militia members, some of whom came to "observe" the rally, carried fully kitted AR15s and various other weapons.

The scene was one of impending doom in one of Virginia's most progressive and scenic cities.

Those who had come to protest against the Unite the Right group were also there, some also carrying sticks. By midmorning, the counterprotestors were joined by civil rights activists, residents of Charlottesville, and local church members. The air was thick as chants between the groups could be heard, alternating between those on the right chanting, "Our blood is soil," and, "Jews will not replace us" with those on the left singing, "This little light of mine, I'm gonna let it shine."

In the middle of the two groups was the militia force I mentioned, that had begun to form in the park. They were dressed in camouflage and were armed for battle. They said they were there to keep the peace. Their presence was felt by everyone. Most did not feel at peace with their presence.

By 10:30, the groups had grown restless. It was only a matter of time before their angst would turn into violence. Some pushing and shoving had started, as did shouting at one another. As tensions boiled, Unite the Right members took up shields and began waving their sticks as they moved toward the Market Street entrance to Emancipation Park. Charlottesville Police Chief Al Thomas Jr. had said the plan was to come into the park through only one entrance, but rally goers abandoned that strategy, which meant the protesters and counterprotesters were not separated from one another. As the Unite the Right made their way toward the entrance of the park, counterprotesters formed a line to block their path. Both sides swung sticks and shot pepper spray at one another as the groups met in the street.

The chaos turned deadly when twenty-year-old James Fields Jr. drove his car through a crowd on the downtown pedestrian mall and killed thirty-two-year-old Heather Heyer. Those streets were supposed to have been closed to traffic during the rally.

While police were in the vicinity, they did not engage the protesters. They were not in riot gear, and as the police chief later said, sending his men into such a fight "would be putting the public law enforcement in jeopardy."

I have reviewed thousands of pages of documents, witness statements, and video evidence concerning the unrest, and I believe that Governor McAuliffe gave a stand-down order to law enforcement, principally to the Virginia State Police. And there is plenty of circumstantial evidence to prove it. The clearest evidence of a stand-down order in Charlottesville is the fact that the police stood down. These facts require you to adopt one of two beliefs: First, hundreds of police officers independently decided that they were too cowardly to uphold their oath to the United States Constitution. Or second, and much more likely, they were simply following orders. The question was never whether there was a stand-down order. It was about who gave it—the state or the city. As a result, the Charlottesville police chief commanded his law enforcement to stand down while hundreds of white supremacists and their sympathizers assaulted and seriously injured counterprotesters, making the police, their chief, and others accessories and facilitators of unconstitutional hate crimes.

The chief has disputed the stand-down orders, but it was quite obvious that they were commanded not to do anything to help those being pummeled and hurt that day. Most police officers wouldn't do that unless they were commanded to act in such a way. The officers on the ground had to be following orders, and those orders led to chaos on Charlottesville's normally tranquil streets. It was the state that created the danger when they brought two violently oppositional groups together and then refused to perform basic law-enforcement duties, preferring rather to watch innocent people be beaten.

Robert Sanchez Turner, a young African-American man, was just one victim assaulted by white supremacists that day in Charlottesville and the law failed to keep him safe. He was beaten senseless by white-supremacist protesters. He suffered neck and head pain from being hit by canes and bottles, some filled with cement, as well as blurred vision from being exposed to tear gas.

Officers were within ten feet of the assault and didn't do anything to stop or apprehend Turner's assailants. The state police stood down, watched it happen, and just turned away. Nexus Derechos Humanos filed a lawsuit (*Turner v. Charlottesville*) on his behalf against the City of Charlottesville, the Charlottesville police chief, and Virginia State Superintendent Colonel W. Steven Flaherty. In our suit we alleged that the defendants enabled hate crimes and that our client's constitutional rights under the Fourteenth Amendment were violated. When we filed our lawsuit on behalf of our client, we referenced a confidential memo to City Manager Jones dated August 24, in which the city council demanded an explanation for the "apparent unwillingness of officers to directly intervene during overt assaults captured by many videos."

Although the lawsuit was filed naming Robert Sanchez Turner as the plaintiff, we funded the litigation on behalf of every person—regardless of race or affiliation—who experienced a beating or a physical assault while the police stood by and didn't do anything.

The government's inaction violated the protesters' constitutional rights.

We lost this case in court because the court said the police don't have any duty to protect citizens. The court's ruling said, "Acting under Pinder's teaching that state actors may not be held liable for 'standing by and doing nothing when suspicious circumstances dictated a more active role for them.'"[10] The Supreme Court ruled that police do not have a duty to affirmatively protect you. The police have a duty to investigate and assist in the prosecution of crimes, but there is no duty to jump in and save you from "merely suspicious circumstances." This is settled law across the United States and is referenced in the state's pleadings in our case.

In this case, the court found an active race riot to be a mere suspicious circumstance. Maybe this will help you understand my vendetta against hypocrisy. If a race riot is a mere suspicious circumstance, what on earth would ever require any police officer to do anything or help anybody? The state didn't even try to deny the stand-down order in their responses to our lawsuit. Their argument was they don't have to protect the people. And the court said they were right. I hated losing this case because we were 100 percent correct, but the law didn't care. We stood up to fight to prove the existence of the actual stand-down order. They stood up to fight to say it didn't matter because they don't have the duty to protect us. We never got to fight our fight because the court decided the state was right. They simply have no duty to protect us.

Such is the life of civil rights activists and attorneys, realizing that the losses, in exposing the systems guttural corruption, can and must be most important in bringing about long-term change.

Even so, an independent review of the actions of law enforcement and city officials was critical of the Charlottesville police as well as the state police for failing to stand up and protect human life. The Charlottesville city attorney, the city manager, and the police chief all left their positions.

Frustrated by the outcome, we decided to appeal and take our case to the US Supreme Court. Our argument is that the state created the danger. In doing that, our attorneys have to prove the stand-down order was an affirmative act by the police that actually caused the riot. From our point of view, the city and state created the problem by bringing the protesters to a larger space in Charlottesville. The original plan was to protest in McIntire Park, but someone from the city decided to steer them to Emancipation Park. When they got everything set up, they effectively said, "not our problem."

For us to win, the United States Supreme Court would have had to agree the state and city acted to create the issue by bringing violent protestors together and then refusing to correct their error. Here's what I mean. As a police officer, if you witness someone being stabbed, you can say, "I don't have a duty to interact or intervene," and you'd be right. If, however, you brought the serial killer in the back of your police car, let him out, and he stabs someone, you have an obligation to intervene because you created the situation.

Robert Sanchez Turner showed up to protest, something any American should be able to do. He saw police officers on horseback, in cars, and in tanks and, therefore, had every reason to believe he was safe in the park where they told him to go and where they corralled him on one side and the white supremacists on the other. The police officers lifted the gates.

It was a set-up.

From the start, the state and city didn't want the protest in Virginia because they knew it was going to end badly. They fought to keep Richard Spencer from having his protest. They tried to deny him his permit, even taking the case to Judge Moore in the Western District of Virginia, who said they had to allow the protest. So they took their case to the fourth circuit, a very conservative court, and they, too, supported Richard Spencer's right to hold the rally. The ACLU represented Spencer in this fight and won. He has a first amendment right to speak. He can protest. The city of Charlottesville was wrong to deny him a permit. And so Richard Spencer's Unite the Right rally happened, leading Charlottesville to race riots and bedlam in the heart of the city.

The state's reaction was a big, "I told you so." They knew it was going to be bad and didn't want to get their hands dirty. It was a childish temper tantrum by the governor of the Commonwealth of Virginia and his superintendent of the state police. It was terrifying and a tempest in a bottle. The mayhem lasted nearly forty-eight hours, and many wondered if this was a precursor of the race riots that were coming.

Would these types of protests break out in other cities? Luckily, they didn't. Not then anyway.

Looking back, Charlottesville should have been wiser, smarter, and more prepared for what was yet to come. The city should have responded as needed, set up parameters, had extra police, and, above all, had a plan. But they didn't. They just thought they could shut it down. When they couldn't, they stepped back and let the two sides fight.

This is a game that has been played many times in America. We had this problem long before Charlottesville. Worse, we've known we have a problem, but the system has always been more important than the individual. In order to preserve the system, the government knows it has to let individuals fight, even if sometimes you have to set up those fights and then walk away while people kill each other.

That's what they did in Charlottesville.

Charlottesville is the most liberal city in Virginia. It shouldn't have happened there or anywhere. As a progressive, it disgusted me because it was an example of everything I loathe about "the ends justify the means" philosophy that liberals far too often adopt. Liberals aren't alone in this. Consider religious conservatives supporting Trump because they get something out of it. It leads to a place of absolute hell because the ends don't justify the means. You can't separate a good result from evil acts. Charlottesville not only let this happen, they set it up. The local government was right in not wanting racists on the city streets of Charlottesville. However, they were wrong in how they went about achieving their desired result, to shut down the rally. They didn't like the message and wanted to shut it down. I also don't like the message, but I believe the best way to expose its ignorance is to let people hear it. By employing the strategy of cancelling the permits after issuing them and then trying to move the rally, the city lit the match that sparked a race riot in America. Seeing this travesty in my home state was a defining moment for me. But it happens all the time in government. Large bureaucracy doesn't solve problems; it creates them. And, to be certain, leadership does it all the time, by design, as a way of force and control. For me, I realized that government is not the solution to our problems. It is often the cause of them.

Before the Korean War, if we wanted to fight a sworn enemy, we would "declare" war against them. To accomplish this, the government would convene Congress, debate the decision, there would be a vote, and then there would be a declaration per the Constitution and the American people would go to war. The reason the power to declare war is bestowed upon Congress is that the founders thought if the situation was ever that desperate, American moms and dads would prefer to have their congressmen vote for such a thing. That way, the American people would be truly vested.

Around the time of the Korean War, we decided to call these declarations "police actions" instead of "war." This afforded a great power to the executive branch without the oversight of Congress, under the idea that we needed to be more agile. It's a pretty high bar to declare war for a reason. But we now allow our presidents to engage in war without the oversight. The Korean War, Vietnam, the Gulf War, the second Gulf War, and the invasions of Afghanistan and Grenada were not wars. We didn't declare war in any of those cases. Calling these police actions gave the president incredible power and control—not unlike a king instead of an elected official.

We won World War I and World War II doing it the right way. Why couldn't we have fought the Korean War or Vietnam using the same process? Had we followed the protocol and made the case to the American people, perhaps we would not have ended up in either of those places. Sadly, we got here because the American people aren't as truly vested as the founders had hoped. If the vote had been given to the people, do you really believe we would have gone to Vietnam or any of the other actions that we had to endeavor to create new propaganda? Instead, we radically weaponized and empowered the presidency of the United States.

When it comes to war, the president has the power in limited instances to respond militarily. Sure, we could enter into minor military skirmishes and the president, as the commander in chief, could guide us out of troubled waters, but we couldn't invade a country without due process. I believe if the government wants to go to war and kill 20,000 to 100,000 American men and women, then they have the responsibility to convince the American people that we should go to war and that the ends justify the means. Of course, the result of no oversight has been a consolidation of power and control in the government in every area since the 1950s, advent of post-World War II.

Governments have used propaganda for centuries to purposely form its citizens opinions during times of war. While carefully designed posters, films, press releases, and even statues have been successfully used to get the public behind war, dishonesty and hypocrisy associated with propaganda often has the opposite effect. Even when it works, the costs to society makes this type of messaging a questionable tool to advance a social cause. Effective propaganda certainly allows governments to frame a specific issue the way they want it supported. Nazi Germany introduced a believable, albeit deadly, propaganda campaign that persuaded German citizens they were the master race and that Jews (and other groups) must be eradicated. To accomplish this, Joseph Goebbels, the Nazis' minister for public enlightenment and propaganda, created anti-Semitic films and commissioned twenty radio stations to broadcast Nazi Germany's message to neighboring nations. As a result of this campaign, over six million people tragically died.

While Adolf Hitler and his regime were using anti-Semitic propaganda that made the "Final Solution" inevitable, America was using a different kind of wartime propaganda to justify its involvement in the war. If you look back to World War II, there were cartoons with racist imagery teaching children that German and Japanese people were bad. Fred Korematsu was a Japanese-American civil rights activist who fought against the internment of Japanese Americans during World War II. After the Japanese bombed Pearl Harbor, President Roosevelt issued an order authorizing the removal of people of Japanese descent living on the West Coast. His order allowed Japanese Americans to be taken from their homes and placed in internment camps. Fred Korematsu challenged that order by filing an appeal, *Korematsu v. United States*.[11] Fred Korematsu was convicted of failing to follow military orders to report to a concentration camp for relocation. The Supreme Court upheld his conviction and stated the internment order was legal.

Forty years later, the U.S. District Court overturned this decision when it was disclosed that evidence had been withheld by the US government during wartime that would have challenged the necessity of imprisoning Korematsu. His crime? Being of Japanese ancestry.

Think it can't happen today? You'd be wrong.

Stories like this are happening every day in our underserved communities. The government wants to pick who the winners and losers are in our country. The government wants us to believe it's us versus them, except the us and the them are never the government. The elites sit on a safe perch and watch the destruction of the American people, while relishing in their shredding of our Constitution.

The elites on both sides do it, and the elites on both sides are wrong.

Americans must wake up!

We are at war—and it is between our government and us.

Just as they've done in wars past, our government uses its manipulation skillset and propaganda against you and me to create "wedge issues," divisions between people based on race, religion, and social issues. Propaganda has become more specific to issues that enable the government to regulate the American people as opposed to controlling a foreign adversary. After World War II, we began to see the United States government use these strategies for manipulation against communities within our country.

Why? So it can control us.

Perhaps the government propaganda we encounter today doesn't pit us against one another as it once pitted us against our foreign enemies. But it plays us against one another. The struggle has become internal and worse, we are doing this to ourselves. Where we used to have united American propaganda against a common enemy, we now drive wedges between American people. The government uses those wedge issues to build large campaign funds and coffers and to garner reactionary votes.

Nowadays, our conflicts are being fought in the streets across America, not on foreign soil. And this isn't a new phenomenon. Around the 1960s, in response to the civil rights movement, African-American communities began pushing for their rights, while the federal and state governments became very protectionist, realizing that even after you achieve a goal and are able to make what would be viewed as positive strides, racism didn't go away. It just found a different way to penetrate the system. And that's why qualified immunity was created.

The same holds true when it comes to same-sex marriage. In 2015, the Supreme Court ruled that the US Constitution provides same-sex couples the right to marry, handing a historic victory to the American gay-rights movement. That decision didn't change how people who opposed gay marriage viewed it. It only changed how they responded to the decision: bakeries refused to make wedding cakes, businesses refused service, and hate crimes against the LGBTQ community increased.

Immigration is a perfect example of our government being at war with an issue. Immigration isn't really the problem the Democrats or Republicans make it out to be. It really is more of a commodity—nothing more, nothing less. I see this every day in the work that I do. Through different factions, the government has used propaganda and hyperbole to inflame the temperatures on both sides and further push people to the extreme.

Capitalists believe that the market economies need consumers. Liberals feel the same way for different reasons. The only people who are naturally anti-immigration are protectionists. It's an incredibly small group, but it has taken over the Republican party.

How? Hysteria by design!

It's the president saying, "Mexico sends its rapists and murderers," while people on the left will proclaim that the right is racist. To an immigrant who doesn't know any better, they believe the government is there to protect them. And, of course, that is not the case. The government is not actually willing to take that duty on. So, instead, they find ways to manipulate us into turning against one another. It's a game designed to lead us to a place where we're so busy fighting that we don't realize who the real enemy is, the one who is taking away our money, our rights, and our humanity. They're doing it by further increasing these hyperbolic claims and driving issues to extremes—and people to the edges of the margins.

When you push people to the edge, you get to keep your power, control, and money. And that's the whole point. Believe me when I say, the people in Congress are not walking the halls fighting about immigration the way the people on Main

Street USA do. And that's exactly the point. For our politicians, it's just business. If you are a liberal Democrat, you've got to be pro-immigration if you're trying to raise money and gain votes. And, if you're a conservative Republican, you've got to be anti-immigration for the same reasons. That's how it works.

As someone who is extremely proud of the work that I do around issues of immigration, I can also understand the anti-immigration position. I don't share it, but I do understand that for the most part, it comes from a place of deep fear. That's why someone like Pat Buchanan is more relevant today than he ever was because his ideology has taken over the leadership of the Republican party in a way that I thought it never would. Absent the economic arguments for immigration, the reality is, anytime you rip a child from its mother's arms, there is a consideration about what to do with that child. We don't have to be afraid to be human beings, and we certainly shouldn't be afraid to follow the direction of Jesus of Nazareth in this regard. And, if you're a capitalist, you get the benefit of huge consumer growth and the visibility of reducing shadow communities. Bringing families out of the shadows and turning them into consumers only supports economic growth. Does it expand the competition pool? Perhaps, but that's the idea of capitalism. And it is humane. It is consistent with the values of America. We know that we need not fear migrants seeking a better life. By bringing people out of the shadows we can make it harder for terrorist groups to try to use our border as a method of planning future attacks. Shadow communities make us less safe, and the establishment of them is simply not consistent with who we are.

Perhaps there was always some form of this abuse of power in the country, but one thing I know for sure is we are a government that was built of, by, and for the people. It was founded on and focused on *limited* power. When the government says something, it carries a lot of weight. And now, those weapons that were once aimed solely at our enemies are brought to bear against the American people on fringe issues, where we the people are pushed to the extremes.

Here's what I mean: When the leadership of this country inflames the fire—not through anything they are doing, but by what they say combined with what they *aren't* doing—horrible situations are created and left to just play out. It's all a plot. The more effective the government is, the harder it is to bring those communities back together and, therefore, the harder it will be to overcome the government. Not only do they *know* that, but it's *why* they're doing it.

And when it comes from the top, as we saw in Lafayette Square with the protestors being tear-gassed and strong-armed, it becomes a powder keg. The president threw matches at it every day to accelerate, elevate, and provoke a response so that he could then watch it burn.

But, of course, we've seen this type of abuse of power many times in our country's history.

Two events in recent history where the government took a knee and ended up abusing its power occurred in Ruby Ridge, Idaho, and Waco, Texas.

The siege at Ruby Ridge involved the infamous shootout between Randy Weaver and his family and federal agents on August 21, 1992, and lasted eleven days. Randy Weaver and his family moved from Iowa to northern Idaho near the Canadian border to escape what they thought was an increasingly corrupt world. They wanted to live off the grid. Randy was a former factory worker and Army Green Beret. He and his wife, Vicky, were religious fundamentalists who distrusted the government and believed the end of the world was near. They moved to the secluded area known as Ruby Ridge so they could homeschool their children and essentially be left alone. The Weavers were known to associate with members of the Aryan Nations, though they themselves were not members. While they held racial separatist beliefs, they were not involved in any violent activity or rhetoric.

In 1985, the FBI and the Secret Service began investigating Weaver for alleged threats he had made against President Ronald Reagan and other government officials. The government agencies believed he had stockpiled weapons—which was his right—and that he was a member of the white-supremacist group Aryan Nations, which Weaver denied. At the time, there were no charges filed against him.

The Bureau of Alcohol, Tobacco, and Firearms, also known as ATF, became aware of the Weavers in 1986 when Randy was introduced to an undercover ATF informant at a meeting at the World Aryan Congress. The informant said he was a weapons dealer. Over the course of the next three years, Weaver and the informant met several times. In 1989, Weaver invited the informant to his home to discuss forming a group to fight the "Zionist Organized Government," his reference to the United States government.

The ATF had originally been investigating Frank Kumnick, who was a friend of Weavers and known to associate with members of the Aryan Nations. Weaver had grown suspicious of the informant and accused him of being a spy for the police. He had been warned by an FBI informant by the name of Rico Valentino. Both agencies were heavily investigating the activities in this region, but especially around the Aryan Nations. By 1989 the undercover ATF agent claimed that Weaver sold him illegal sawed-off shotguns. To avoid charges, the agent offered Weaver the chance to become an informant on the Aryan Nations, which Weaver turned down. When he refused to become an informant, he was indicted for making and keeping illegal weapons. He was released on bail and awaited his trial, which was set for February 20, 1991. Unfortunately, his probation officer told Weaver it wasn't until March 20. When he missed his February 20 trial, a warrant was immediately issued for his arrest and noted it might have to be set aside if he showed up on the March 20 date. However, Randy Weaver did not show up in March, and the grand jury indicted him for failing to appear. While the government sent him numerous letters to negotiate their terms, Weaver was still at large, making him a fugitive.

The case was handed over to the United States Marshals Service, which was responsible for finding Weaver and bringing him into custody. The US marshals were well aware of his arsenal and his anti-government beliefs. They were certain he would neither turn himself in nor surrender peacefully. After surveillance teams noticed the Weavers were almost always armed at home, they thought it might make sense to see if they could infiltrate the family by going undercover as their new neighbors, but they never got the chance.

On the morning of August 21, 1992, Deputy Marshal Dave Hunt and Deputy Marshal Art Roderick were discovered by the Weaver's dogs. The dogs, Randy's fourteen-year-old son, Sammy, Randy, and Kevin Harris ran as the surveillance team scattered. A shootout between the Weavers and the marshals ended with Sammy

was just ten years old. He was, by all accounts, sick and perverted. By the time he died, Koresh had as many as twenty wives.

He was reported to be abusive to the children in the sect, disciplining them often, and allegedly with force. There was no heat, electricity, or running water and it was mandatory to attend Bible study three times a day. As a Branch Davidian, you were supposed to separate yourself from the world, its sins, the flesh, and the desires of the world to be spiritual. Koresh urged the use of guns, while preaching about the end of the world. He thought the Branch Davidian's would eventually come under attack by the US government. In preparation, they began stockpiling guns and ammunition.

As with Ruby Ridge, the concerns of ATF and Koresh were based on allegations that the group, considered a distant subsidiary of the Seventh-day Adventist Church, possessed illegal firearms and was conceivably turning AR-15 semiautomatic rifles into machine guns.

Just after 9:00 a.m. on Sunday, February 28, a caravan of eighty vehicles, including two trailers pulled by trucks and loaded with seventy-six heavily armed ATF agents, made its way to the property. The caravan stopped in front of the compound as agents stormed the center. Right around the same time, two Blackhawk helicopters arrived and hovered over the property.

A shootout ensued that left four ATF agents and six Branch Davidians dead. This began the seven-week confrontation that captivated the world.

On the morning of April 19, 1993, federal agents used tanks to shoot tear gas into the Branch Davidian building as a way to force Koresh and his remaining followers to give themselves up. That didn't happen. Instead, a raging fire broke out in several locations in the structure that housed Koresh and others. ATF agents alleged that the sect had started the inferno, while survivors blamed the government for lighting it. A Congressional investigation concluded that Koresh and his followers set the fire themselves. A commonsense review of the videotaped evidence shows a tank plowing into an old building and it catching on fire. You be the judge.

The FBI's tactical experts failed in the way they handled the situation. They couldn't possibly understand that it was David Koresh's religious beliefs that brought him to his fiery and dramatic end. His apocalyptic beliefs were based on the Book of Revelation. In the end, the FBI delivered to David Koresh the apocalypse that he and his followers expected.

Questions remain about the motives behind the ATF raid in Waco.

I think it's safe to say the Branch Davidians were a cult. A cult is where people do things they wouldn't normally do, like living in polygamy or overlooking child sexual abuse. The cult leader is someone who makes you believe they have absolute authority over you, and then they impose strict rules and restrictions and expectations you didn't ask for. I am not saying our country runs like a cult, but when you think about it, as long as you fall in line with whatever the cult leader demands of you, everything is just fine. It's when you step out of that where the problems really begin. If you defy the cult leader, you get punished. If you follow the demands, you are rewarded.

Isn't it time we stop listening to our government as if it were David Koresh?

When the government takes a knee, it's against its responsibility to hold people accountable. It's placing its knee in the back of the individuals who suffer as a result. If you believe you are right and then take action based on that assumption, you do so having faith that others will feel the same as you do. As a result, you will always think the end justifies the means.

If your child were dying, would you break the law if it meant saving him? Probably.

In that moment, the end justifies the means. Sometimes there are consequences for those actions, but there are rarely consequences for the government. If you look at the video of Officer Chauvin with his knee on George Floyd's neck, he believed what he was doing was right. When the officers in Buffalo, New York, knocked an old man down to the ground, they, too, thought what they did was right. These people haven't gone insane. They simply came to believe that the end justified the means.

When you believe that you are 100 percent right, the end will always justify the means. And it simply isn't possible that any government agent is 100 percent right all the time. People are fallible.

The divisions that exist between the American people are provoked by the government on a daily basis. Leaders from both sides of the government create this hysteria on purpose, and hysteria is fear. By creating enough fear, they build walls that can't be overcome in a difficult situation. Many seemingly opposing groups might be naturally united against the power of the government, but they rarely come together on common issues. Groups like Black Lives Matter, Antifa, the Proud Boys, and the militia movement are each formed by very different people, but the one thing they should all agree on is their right to fight tomorrow about issues they disagree on today. These groups represent some of the most active, extreme, and controversial examples, but they make an important point. The back and forth between the state and activists from varying sides may ultimately force a unification of the non-state activists. Should such a union occur before the country descends into violence, it may help prevent a larger civil conflict in the United States. If they are forced to unite against the state after conflict begins, the potential loss of property and life will be breathtaking.

If we don't fight for our rights, when the time comes, there is not going to be anyone around to defend us. We must understand that constitutional liberty shouldn't be seen through the lens of race, religion, or whether you agree with a person or not. Even the worst person you know has rights in this country. And if that person has rights, then you and I do.

We need to protect the rights of the meekest and weakest so they are protected for us all. If one person in this country loses their civil liberties, we all do. If one person can lose their rights, then the rights weren't real to begin with. I was born a free American, and I intend to die as one. Are you willing to lose your civil rights? If not, now is the time to stand up.

9

THE LOPSIDED TRAVESTY OF QUALIFIED IMMUNITY

"QUALIFIED IMMUNITY" IS A PHRASE WE'VE HEARD A LOT ABOUT LATELY. Let's take a good look at what a travesty it is—and a lopsided travesty at that.

In 1870 and 1871, the United States Congress created three laws together known as the Enforcement Acts. The third of them, also known as the Ku Klux Klan Act, codified the civil rights of black people, as enacted in the statutes. This wasn't long after the Civil War, when African Americans were granted emancipation, citizenship rights, and protections in the United States. The Civil Rights Act, as the third one was also called, was designed to criminalize much of the KKK activity by enabling people to file lawsuits when acts of terror were committed against them because of their race.

The third Enforcement Act also created "section 1983," which gave people the right to sue the government. President Ulysses S. Grant signed the act into law as a way to suspend the writ of habeas corpus and combat the KKK and other white-supremacy organizations. Section 1983, however, wasn't recognized until 1961, after *Monroe v. Pape*, a Supreme Court case that involved a black family, the Monroes, who sued the Chicago Police Department.[12] The Chicago police had gone into the Monroes' house without a warrant, rounded them up, made the family stand together naked in the living room, and ransacked every room in their house.

They emptied drawers, ripped open mattresses, cut open sofas, and arrested James Monroe, the patriarch, interrogating him for hours.

Supreme Court Justice William Douglas recognized the Civil Rights Act, allowing them to sue the officers for violating their constitutional rights. The very purpose of the Civil Rights Act was to give remedy to parties deprived of constitutional rights.

Six years later, in 1967, the doctrine of qualified immunity was created as a way to keep African Americans from having access to the courts, even though the Fourteenth Amendment guarantees that very right. At first, qualified immunity was invented to be a modest exception for public officials who had acted in good faith and who believed that their conduct was lawful. When the courts began to experience larger numbers of cases filed under the Civil Rights Act that took away power from the police state, the Supreme Court intervened by creating qualified immunity. The court stated it wanted to protect police officers from bankruptcy, but they were really protecting police officers from us. To fall under its protection, all a police officer needs to say is that he thought what he was doing was the right thing. It doesn't matter how egregious the act. It simply doesn't matter.

Think about this: We passed a law in 1871 that conferred rights that were not recognized until 1961, and then six years later the court invalidated those rights by establishing qualified immunity. That means African Americans—in fact all of us—were really only allowed to sue the police for violating our rights from 1961 to 1967.

When Rodney King was arrested in Los Angeles for drunk driving, the police officer said he believed he was on PCP and, thus, needed to be restrained. At the time, under orders from Chief of Police Daryl Gates, the LAPD had been practicing drills and trained to learn different choke holds, only to be used if the perpetrator was on PCP. As it turned out, Rodney King was not on drugs; he was drunk. The officers beat him mercilessly, hitting him with their batons somewhere between fifty-three and fifty-six times and jolting him with 50,000 volts shot from a stun gun. No charges were ever filed against King. Four officers were eventually tried on charges of use of excessive force. Of these, three were acquitted, and the jury failed to reach a verdict on one charge for the fourth.

Within hours of the verdict, riots in the streets of Los Angeles ensued. Over the course of six days, sixty-three people were killed and nearly 2,400 injured. The rioting came to an end when California called in the National Guard and the president ordered the United States Army and Marine Corps to restore order.

Sound familiar?

These types of encounters have been taking place for decades in America. There's nothing new about what we saw after the killing of George Floyd, Breonna Taylor, and Rayshard Brooks. The questions are: When will it end? And will it end before the proverbial straw has broken that camel's back? Or have we just witnessed that?

Qualified immunity was meant to reduce the number of cases that would be brought by black people in the dawn of the new post-civil rights movement arena. The 1960s was a very tumultuous time in our country. African Americans gained a lot of liberties through statue and court rulings. The doctrine of qualified immunity basically holds public officials, not just police, to a much lower standard than you or I are held to because they can only be held accountable insofar as where they violate a clearly established right in light of existing case law.

What this means is that police, in particular, get cases dismissed all the time. The Supreme Court said that qualified immunity protects, "all but the plainly incompetent or those who knowingly violate the law."

That's bad enough. Why should police be held to that unrestrictive of a standard? Worse, in order to find a clearly established right, what the courts have determined is that the violation of your rights has to be consistent with a prior case where an officer was found to have violated those rights. Qualified immunity says that unless that exists, the case must be dismissed.

If you hire a contractor, give him a deposit, and he never showed up again, you would want your day in court, right? If you hired a lawyer and they don't show up in court, you'd want satisfactory remedy to that too. Well, qualified immunity lets public officials, including the police, completely off the hook. Sorry, you lose. As it turned out, qualified immunity is an exception to the Ku Klux Klan Act and to the Civil Rights Act. It was nothing more than a tool to specifically terrorize and to make terrorizing black people in America legal.

Fifteen years after qualified immunity was created, in 1982, the Supreme Court dramatically expanded it. In *Harlow v. Fitzgerald*, they said that the protection that was afforded to police and public officials would no longer be based on whether they acted in good faith.[13] Even those who maliciously violate people's rights are immune unless the victim can show that his or her right was "clearly established."

But there is no case law to consistently establish what clearly established rights are.

The court said that in order to show that a law is clearly established, the victim must show a prior case that involves, "the same specific context and particular conduct." Unless the victim can point out a case where the court has decided that liability is established with some "specific context," and the same "particular conduct," the officer shall be shielded from liability.

This was a death blow to the constitutional rights of the American people. Most didn't even know it happened. We certainly didn't know that a case from 1982 would lead to America burning in 2020. However, if you really step back and think about it, the con that qualified immunity represents, which has been perpetrated against the American people, is an offense that contextualizes just how determined America's elites are to maintain absolute power and control.

When you hear African Americans talking about not getting the rights they were promised, they're right. They got the promise, and the police received the exception. There's a thin blue line that covers a multitude of sin.

According to a Stanford study reported by *The New York Times*, more than 90 percent of state and federal criminal convictions are the result of pleading guilty, even if those people maintain they didn't commit the crime. And the Department of Justice Office of the Inspector General report at any given time in the United States, approximately 630,000 Americans are locked up in local jails. Of those, 70 percent are waiting for their cases to go to trial. In the end, most of those people will plead guilty, waiving their right to a trial, even if they didn't commit the crime.

This broken criminal justice system is a symptom of mass incarceration. More than ten million people, or one person every three seconds, are arrested every year in America. The bulk are for victimless crimes, drug violations, and low-level offenses.

Imagine for a moment if every single person who was arrested decided to take their case to trial.

Here's what that would look like.

Low-income people are less likely to afford bail, which means the majority of the jailed population is made up of people whose detention stems from being poor. Ironically, the left's war against bail bondsmen will leave no one to help people afford what are already onerous amounts. This will mean scores more people incarcerated over the next several years.

People in jail are more likely to plead guilty because it is typically the fastest track to getting out of jail.

By design, plea bargains are supposed to be a way of avoiding lengthy, costly trials for defendants who are clearly guilty. Instead, they've become a way for low-income people to get out of jail as quickly as possible, even if it means pleading guilty to a crime they didn't commit.

There's a growing understanding that the problems of policing are not about a few high-profile deaths, but are the result of *over*-policing, a much bigger and powerful reason. And, to be certain, there are profound political agendas to use policing to solve every social problem, especially in poor communities and communities of color.

The result of all of this is even worse than the abuse of power by the police state. It becomes an infringement on the Fourth, Fifth, Sixth, Seventh, Eighth, and Fourteen Amendments. It means the police have a right to come and search your things and a judge can deny your motion to exclude, making it easier to convict you. It also impacts your right to due process and the right to a speedy trial by an impartial jury of the state or district where the crime was supposed to have been committed.

Obviously, qualified immunity rips all of these rights away from the victim.

The Sixth Amendment ("the right to a speedy and public trial, by an impartial jury") guarantees a process, and it guarantees rights. The amendment is violated when anyone's right to a speedy trial is compromised. Sadly, our right to a jury trial is abridged every day. The plea-bargaining system, the overcharging system, and the incredible power of prosecutors to leverage multiple charges to convince a person to plead guilty all prevent the accused from getting a jury trial. All of those easily become violations of the Sixth Amendment, and that impacts all of us—except when a police officer commits a crime. That police office gets more rights than you and I would. He also gets better representation than the courts provide.

How does this happen? The prosecutor is the officer's lawyer, and the prosecutor gets to go in front of the grand jury to explain himself. He doesn't worry about having to obtain witnesses in his favor because he's the only witness talking to the grand jury. It's his word versus yours.

This, too, is a violation of the spirit of the Sixth Amendment rights, if not the letter. When police have super police powers and zero accountability, people die at the hands of police—and they have unions to cover it up.

Police must be criminally prosecuted, and we all must be afforded all of the rights granted by the Sixth Amendment when we are accused of committing a crime. We must all be on equal footing. The police should not have super rights. If they do, they will surely abuse them. If you want to give everyone the same rights the police have, then great. I'll take that option. No one gets arrested, and everyone lives and dies by the same standard. However, our status quo clearly reeks of hypocrisy.

In post-COVID America, the speedy trial rights of the accused are being violated more and more every day. People are being held in jail longer than they should be under the speedy trial rules. Many more abuses are happening around the plea-bargaining system, power the prosecutors use to compel people not to exercise their right to a jury trial.

This abuse of power will continue to linger long after the threat of COVID has come and gone if we aren't careful. There's great danger in that. If we continue to criminalize daily life in America, more people will be affected.

And, as I found out at a young age, once you are involved in the criminal process, you have to hire lawyers, you have to go to court, and you become a part of the criminal-justice system. Only then can you truly understand how abusive that system is.

The Seventh Amendment ("The right of trial by jury shall be preserved, and no fact tried by a jury, shall be otherwise re-examined") is deeply connected to these abuses as well. If you have a lawsuit that you want to bring against someone for more than twenty dollars, you have a right to a jury. Everything tried by a jury must follow the laws of the United States or the rules of common law. You can't restrict a person's right to take a suit to trial—and that is exactly what qualified immunity does. It strips our right to bring suits at common law to a jury trial, because when a case is dismissed under qualified immunity, there is no jury trial. There's no trial at all!

The Eighth Amendment ("Excessive bail shall not be required, nor excessive fines imposed, nor cruel and unusual punishments inflicted") guarantees freedom from excessive bail and cruel and unusual punishment. Our founders thought it important to make sure that bail that is excessive, or the pretrial detention of innocent persons, should be precluded.

How far have we come from that liberty principle?

Let me share another story that means a lot to me.

On February 14, 2018, fourteen students and three members of the staff were murdered at Marjory Stoneman Douglas High School in Parkland, Florida. The shooter was a former student, Nikolas Cruz.

A few weeks later, his younger brother, Zach, went to the high school while it was still closed, trying to reconcile what his brother had done. He and Nikolas shared the same mother and were both adopted as children. Both of their adoptive parents were dead, and at the time of the shooting, they only had each other.

Zach skateboarded around the school, trying to make sense of the tragedy that had taken place just a few weeks earlier. A police officer on the campus stopped Zach to question him. He told the officer he was trying to take it all in because he didn't understand why his brother would commit such a horrific mass murder. He said he felt his life was upside down and he needed to be there.

The police officer didn't understand. He felt as though he needed to detain Zach. *What if he was a killer too?* While that may have been relevant, there was no legal basis on which to detain him. The only thing Zach did wrong that day was trespass. Nonetheless, the police arrested him and took him to jail.

Why? Because he was the brother of the Parkland shooter.

Was this relevant? Yes, of course.

Was it necessary? Absolutely not.

The charge was a Class 2 misdemeanor for trespassing. The statute in Florida states that the bond for such as charge is twenty-five dollars and up to fifteen days in jail as an ultimate sentencing if it is a very serious trespassing offense.

Someone posted the twenty-five dollars for Zach at ten o'clock that night. And just around the same time, Captain Sherena Green went to the judge and asked if he would issue an order to hold Zach. While we could never find an order from the judge, Green and jail leadership did not release Zach even though he had paid his bail and was not being held on a legitimate warrant.

This was unconstitutional.

Such a move was intentional and, therefore, rose above the mere negligence required to maintain deliberate indifference to his right to be released.

I am not even sure the order actually exists because I've never seen a copy of it. If it was a verbal order, it was not valid. What the order did, however, was allow the judge to set his bond at $500,000. Prosecutors argued for the higher bail because they became concerned after a conversation they had with Zach where he mentioned his brother's notoriety and a fan club that could attract girls. Zach was given a mental health evaluation and authorities searched his home for weapons under a new law that was passed after the Parkland shooting.

No weapons were found.

A bail of $500,000 ought to offend all of our sensibilities as Americans and our understanding of what it means to have due process and the right to liberty pending a trial for accusations we're not yet convicted of. There is simply no argument to justify a half-a-million-dollar bond for a twenty-five-dollar misdemeanor charge.

Clearly, the authorities in Broward County conspired to hold him in custody.

Zach couldn't post the new bond, so he sat in a Broward County jail with people who were charged with extreme and violent crimes being given smaller bonds than that. This was the only time in state history where a Class 2 misdemeanor trespassing bond was higher than $50,000.

The prosecutors in Florida took Zach's liberty away without any right to do so whatsoever because, to them, the end justified the means. They created unreasonable fear with no plan, no results, and an abdication of liberty that didn't solve the problem. Locking him up only compounded the problem for him and the community. It was unfair and unjust. Still, someone thought it was worth it not to risk another shooting.

As a result, Zach had to accept what ultimately happened to him, which was two weeks of some of the most indescribable time in jail any human being could endure. We allege the authorities engaged in a campaign of intimidation and torture once Zach was in the Broward main jail facility. He was subjected to sleep-deprivation tactics, where guards would repeatedly wake him at all hours, he had to wear a restraint vest at all times, and he had an intense light shining on him twenty-four hours a day, creating sensory deprivation. He had a guard standing next to him 24/7. They never left him, so he was under one-on-one direct supervision. The guard constantly stared at him and wouldn't speak. Zach was quickly placed on suicide watch and suffered immeasurably as a result.

This treatment clearly violated his Fourteenth Amendment rights to due process.

Given the impossibly high bail, coupled with dehumanizing treatment in jail, Zach was ultimately and unjustly forced to accept a guilty plea just to escape the horrors of custody in the Broward Main Jail facility for ten days. He was placed on six months' probation after pleading no contest.

This is where this story gets personal.

I was so moved by Zach's story that NDH decided to represent him pro bono. I wanted the people responsible for detaining and mistreating him to be held accountable. There was no question the Broward County sheriff's office had to change, and that change needed to be comprehensive. The way inmates are treated in jail, especially at the Broward Main jail, must change as well.

We filed a lawsuit against the Broward Sheriff's Office, the State Attorney's Office, and the county judge who set Zach's bond for the heavy-handed treatment after his arrest.

While I was there to fight for Zach, upon meeting him, he instantly became a part of our family. He became like a son to me, as if I had raised him from birth. And, last year, he asked to be adopted by my partner and me.

I honestly consider the honor of having a chance to help raise Zach to be one of the most amazing gifts that I've ever received. We have continued to fight for Zach, as, ultimately, he settled with the Broward Sheriff's office. He is happier today because he fought abusive law enforcement in Broward County and won. And he is a free person because he stood up and fought for his freedom.

Still, had he not settled, we would have struggled to recover anything at all or even reach a trial—because of qualified immunity, which would have protected the police and the system that violated his constitutional rights.

In the courts, there are very few tools for the lawyers to challenge qualified immunity. Despite national public outcry, protests, and the burning of our cities around the country, the Supreme Court has rejected any notion of revisiting qualified immunity, a doctrine it itself created. The court utterly refused to hear the case of Norman Cooper, a thirty-three-year-old black father, who died at his parent's home after being tased nine times by two San Antonio, Texas, police officers in 2015. Cooper's family filed a claim of excessive force; however, the Fifth Circuit US Court of Appeals decided the officers had qualified immunity and wouldn't have to answer for their actions. That decision is final, as this was one of ten cases involving qualified immunity that the Supreme Court had examined for possible review in spring 2020, but ultimately it was rejected.

Nevertheless, there is hope. On June 19, 2020, also known as Juneteenth, the State of Colorado abolished qualified immunity. It was a fitting day for such a landmark law, the day commemorating the freeing of the slaves. The Enhanced Law

Enforcement Integrity Act also calls for an end to the use of chokeholds and deadly force for nonviolent crimes. State reform isn't a complete substitute for federal abolition of laws, but it is a good start.

The vast majority of law-enforcement operations—and law-enforcement abuses—are conducted by state and local police. State governments can address their misdeeds without waiting for either the Supreme Court or Congress to act. Michigan Representative Justin Amash, an independent, announced his intention to introduce legislation that would end qualified immunity for law enforcement across the country. He, like many, believe that it is time for Congress to "correct" the "mistake" of the Supreme Court by passing his bill to abolish qualified immunity for officers.

New Jersey Senator Cory Booker and Massachusetts Senator Ed Markey, both Democrats, announced their intention to push for qualified immunity reform in the Senate. Senator Booker said, "Cities are literally on fire with the pain and anguish wrought by the violence visited upon black and brown bodies. There's no one singular policy change that will fix this issue tomorrow. We need an entire set of holistic reforms to improve police training and practices and ensure greater accountability and transparency."[14]

He is correct.

Colorado is a model of what can be accomplished and what would serve as a terrific blueprint for what can be done. And while that is progress, change is not happening fast enough. How many lives will it take to wake up to the lopsided travesty of qualified immunity? There are decades of horror that have been brought on the African-American community because of this injustice.

Sure, we live in desperate times, and desperate times, they say, call for desperate measures. But if those desperate measures include suspending liberty interests, then we had no liberty interests in the first place. Liberty interests always matter, and they matter most during desperate times. Is liberty supposed to matter only when it isn't tested by crisis?

If you believe the idea that freedom can be suspended when things get bad, then your freedom is meaningless. Freedom only means something when it means the same thing all the time.

Qualified immunity is the ultimate perversion of liberty in the United States precisely because it creates super-empowered, unaccountable police. The fact that the legal doctrine ever existed is a stain on the history of America. If it continues now that people are cognizant of what it is and why it exists, then we are choosing a not free America.

10

THE BURNING OF PRECINCT THREE

"We must be concerned not merely about who murdered them, but about the system, the way of life, the philosophy which produced the murderers."
—DR. MARTIN LUTHER KING JR.

"I CAN'T BREATHE."

Those were the words of George Floyd who lay dying in the streets of Minneapolis. May 25, 2020, wasn't the first time we as a nation sat in collective awe watching an all too familiar yet horrifying scene. But, at the time, he was the latest victim of our near-zero accountability policy for law enforcement—qualified immunity. Video footage showed a white police officer with his knee pressed firmly against the neck of a handcuffed, unresisting black man. George Floyd's crime? Allegedly attempting to pass a counterfeit $20 bill in a local bodega.

Three other officers stood guard, doing nothing to intervene as George Floyd lay on the ground, slowly dying from asphyxiation.

"I'm comin', Dad!"

Those were the words of fourteen-year-old Sam Weaver, after his dad, Randy, yelled, "Come home, son." Sam had just been shot in the arm by federal agents invading their property.

The cops finished the job, killing Sam.

The family retrieved the body to prepare it for burial. Federal agents waited until Randy and his other children came to pay their last respects to Sam and opened sniper fire on the family. Ultimately, the cops killed Sam, shot Randy, and executed his wife while she stood holding their infant child. Hundreds of federal agents watched the horror, and scores more worked to cover up the crimes committed by the agents at Ruby Ridge.

Those federal agents have never been prosecuted for their crimes.

"I can't breathe."

The same last words uttered by George Floyd were also heard from Eric Garner. On July 17, 2014, Garner was confronted by undercover police on Staten Island and accused of selling untaxed cigarettes. A video of that encounter showed the unarmed Garner resisting the police officers, saying he was tired of being harassed by the police. Officer Daniel Pantaleo, who was white, placed Garner in a chokehold from behind, a move that had been banned by the New York City Police Department. Pantaleo and the other officers wrestled Garner to the ground. From there he could be heard saying, "I can't breathe," until his body went listless.

None of the officers involved was indicted, and it took five years for Pantaleo to be fired in 2019.

"Look out!" (Screams)

Those were the words and sounds captured by FBI listening devices placed inside the Branch Davidian compound in Waco, Texas, when federal agents rammed the building with a tank. This encounter ultimately led to a fire that burned seventy-six people alive, including twenty-five children.

"Don't shoot."

Those, according to several witnesses, were the last words of Michael Brown. He was walking down the street when he was shot to death on August 9, 2014, in Ferguson, Missouri, during an encounter with Darren Wilson, a white Ferguson police officer. Wilson was investigating a shoplifting complaint and claimed Brown matched the description of one of the suspects. According to contemporaneous accounts, Brown had his hands up and told the officer not to shoot, yet he was shot six times. Brown was unarmed.

The officer was not indicted.

"Can't we all just get along?"

Those were the words of Rodney King at a press conference after he had been brutally beaten by fourteen LAPD officers on March 3, 1991. King was apprehended after a high-speed chase and was pummeled during his arrest for drunk driving. The attack on King was caught on film by a civilian bystander. The footage clearly showed King, who was unarmed, on the ground being punched, kicked, knelt on, shot with a stun gun. The outcome of the officer's trial sparked the 1992 Los Angeles Riots, which started in South Central L.A.

The LAPD stood down, believing the situation was too dangerous for their officers to control.

"You're going to kill me...Help me!"

Those were the last words of Tony Limpa, a white man who had called 911 and asked for help because he was having an anxiety attack. He didn't know what was happening and was becoming increasingly agitated. Dallas police responded. This incident occurred in 2016, but it wasn't until civil litigation led to the release of body-cam footage that we heard these horrifying last words. What's worse, we saw a cadre of white and black officers executing a man who called for help. Police had Limpa on the ground for over fourteen minutes. And they didn't just have him on the ground. They had him zip-tied at his hands and feet. Dallas police officer Dustin Dillard kept his knee in Limpa's back while he was in what is called the "prone position"—a controversial police technique that can lead to asphyxiation or, as in the case of Tony Limpa, cardiac arrest.

Tony died while Dallas police officers mocked and made fun of him.

"I want my union rep…"

These are the words of every police officer who has ever faced disciplinary action or accusation that they shot, beat, choked, and killed an unarmed citizen in the country.

Union rules don't allow an officer to talk or provide any information without a union rep present.

Zero accountability for law enforcement is marking a stark rise of fascism in our country, focused on controlling the narrative and silencing the opposition with total domination and force. This is the army of oppression. It is my belief that unless an officer's life is in imminent danger, and no other course of action could prevent the life of that officer or other people from being taken, that law enforcement should never kill an American citizen without that person ever facing a trial and receiving due process. Anytime a police officer shoots someone in the back, it shouldn't even be a conversation about whether their action was justified or not.

But that shouldn't be what happens in our country. We must never give the police the right to execute people on the street. We have to be very specific about what limitations we're going to set on that power.

Why?

The police state is power that can't be checked. Killing someone who has committed a non-violent crime but who has not been convicted of that crime is wrong.

When I first started writing this book, we were in the midst of the first wave of a global pandemic. I worried then about the state of our country, the economy, and the impact of being cooped up for months. I could see that impact in the eyes and hear it in the voices of the victims this was happening to for years and decades, and it was getting louder. When the COVID-19 pandemic hit, I knew, without a doubt, that we were living in a pressure cooker that wouldn't take much to blow it up.

History, especially for black and brown people in America, has a way of repeating itself. Because of that, I suspected there might be an uprising that could radically change the lives of every American and the way we think and force us to pay closer attention to what is happening all around us. It was a tempest in a teapot, and I thought we had more time before it happened.

I was wrong.

The reason I started the *Not Free America* podcast in the midst of our nationwide shutdown was to be the voice for those of us who never feel seen or heard. I wanted to talk about the things people shy away from, especially the very things our government doesn't want us to know, like the expiration of America and the potential for great calamity for her people.

Right after the *Not Free America* podcast launched, I had the chance to see an old friend and fellow minister who reminded me of the beautiful and scary imagery from Revelation chapters 12–14. One night after a podcast, I sat down and re-read the text. In fact, I read Revelation and the Book of Daniel and began to wonder if some crazy version of something once prophesized might be on the horizon.

Let me get something straight. I'm not a literal interpretationist. God chose to give his message through man, with man's limited understanding. This makes total sense…otherwise, we would never know God. We could never perceive God. That's why God gives us prophets, and, in my theology, that's why he gave us Jesus.

Revelation 12 begins with a magnificent vision of a woman floating in the universe, surrounded by celestial bodies. She is pregnant and giving birth. As her child is born, her son is removed from her, and taken to another heavenly place. The woman, who represents the church, is sent to earth. The great serpent, who has the power to move celestial bodies, comes to earth to hunt the woman and torture her.

This is the beginning of the end.

Revelation 13 tells us that governments will unite and prescribed some sort of "mark" that all must take. It is written that you will not be able to buy or sell without this mark.

As a young kid in Pentecostal Sunday School class, I always thought this was ridiculous. I mean, how would a government ever require such a thing when the Bible literally instructs people not to take it. And why does it matter? The day I heard my president say he would use the US military to deliver COVID-19 vaccines all over the country, I wondered, *Might people be socially forced to obtain a potentially risky vaccine?* We are creating a vaccine in a matter of months for a virus similar to the common cold, which we have never been able to vaccinate against. The process of creating and approving a vaccine often takes upwards of ten years, and we are speeding into a year. If that's not risky, what is?

Could you imagine being restricted from buying or selling if you haven't been vaccinated? This is a reality in our world right now, and I realized that maybe Revelation wasn't so ridiculous after all.

A lot of people don't understand that when you read the Book of Revelation, you are reading the words of a man simply called John, possibly the Apostle John. He may have been someone we would now consider a psychotic person. The Roman authorities, who might have considered him a sorcerer and might have been afraid of him, banished him to the Mediterranean island of Patmos, where he ultimately died. But before he died, he wrote the Book of Revelation.

If you understand mental-health issues, you understand that sometimes people who have mental-health issues actually have perceptions that others don't. I think there can be prophets from all walks of life. If John were being divinely or otherwise inspired, and was a prophet given messages, you can only imagine who he would have been seen as in that time, and why he would have written it down. It isn't unreasonable to expect that much of the craziness surrounding post-apocalyptic predictions makes more sense once you strip away the apocalyptic parts. However, the prophecies in Revelation point to a very specific time in human history where all humans will go through a very difficult period.

Has that time of prophecy come?

Not long after my personal spiritual revelation, the country collectively watched in horror at the murder of George Floyd. I have often thought about whether the fact that we were all at home during lockdown made a difference in how we, as a country, and certainly the people of Minneapolis, reacted to what was happening. He wasn't the only black man in America killed by police that day, that week, or that month. There were plenty more we didn't hear about, plenty more we still haven't heard about, and plenty more whose murder was captured on video.

American people have often taken to the streets in protest of the countless black lives lost at the hands of the police: the Birmingham Riot of 1963, the Watts Riots in 1965, the 1967 Detroit Riots, the rioting in 125 American cities that followed the assassination of Dr. Martin Luther King in 1968, and hundreds of protests and riots that followed. All of these lead us to the many we've seen around the country in 2020, including George Floyd, Breonna Taylor, Ahmaud Arbery, and Rayshard Brooks. Every single one of these riots were related to mass racial prejudice and police brutality in the United States.

What was different about the protests in Minneapolis was the presence of so many white people. It wasn't just hippie radicals rallying for peace. *Everyone* was demonstrating for racial equality. They were angry about racism and its victims. We certainly didn't see that during the Rodney King riots. At that time, most white people didn't seem to be willing to put themselves on the frontline to battle racism as they now do. It really isn't racism, however, at least not typically. It is really about what you experience.

White America is finally waking up to the reality of police abuse and the police unions that literally organize against us. This realization is much needed and may just save our Republic.

The day-to-day reality for African Americans in this country is very different than it is for white people.

Why? For one especially important reason: our ancestors established a radical liberty notion in the formation of the United States of America, but African Americans were not a part of that at all.

And when they were finally led into it, we began to change the laws. The turn of the century brought all of the Jim Crow laws, which where were designed to limit the effectiveness of the protections from the Constitution to African Americans.

In some ways, we don't need to return to a liberty principle for African Americans; we need to get there once and for all.

As a nation, we've been responding to the freeing of slaves since Reconstruction. African Americans have never achieved true equal protection or equal access. And to stop them from achieving it, the police state is literally killing them. This rampant systemic abuse isn't new, but it needs to end.

There needs to be a better distinction between what police can do and what they should do.

There's no question the United States has been on a tragic streak for decades, if not centuries, of encounters between law enforcement and black Americans. All we have to do is apply the same liberty principles to everyone—not just some. How do we accomplish this? It's simple: We must give African Americans true access to what the Constitution says, to its guarantees and promises. After hundreds of years of case law based on constructive racism designed to discourage people from being able to bring civil cases, to create bifurcated higher sentencing ranges for African Americans, which we've had for ages, why are we still not getting this right?

The scene in Minneapolis on May 25, 2020, was horrifying. A white officer pressed his knee against the neck of a handcuffed, unresisting black man who was begging him to get off before losing consciousness and dying. There were three other officers standing by, making sure no one came to the aid of George Floyd.

Anytime good officers look the other way, they become bad officers.

If I were to walk past a parked car with a baby locked inside a car on a hot day and not say anything, I would be just as responsible for that child dying as the parent who left the baby in the car. I may not be legally responsible, but my conscience and my heart would know I walked away. If you are aware of a problem and you aren't actively seeking to solve that problem, then you're just like the officers who watched George Floyd die. You either go along with something or you don't.

History judges you based on your actions.

Nexus Derechos Humanos sometimes hires private investigators who come from law enforcement. Every time we interview a candidate, I always ask if they've ever hidden evidence, made up evidence, or concocted a lie to convict the defendant.

Without hesitation, they answer no.

But then I ask them about the last time they knew another officer who did do those things and they didn't report him or her? There's usually an awkward moment of silence before answering with something like, "You have to understand. It's not so black or white," or, "There's a lot of gray," or "It's politics, you know?"

Those answers simply say, "I'm as bad as they are." If you don't care enough to say something when someone's civil rights are being violated, at least go out and have the courage to be true to your own privileged ideology. Police have absolute power, and we all know power corrupts.

Police brutality always brings about calls for change. Whether it's better training, civilian oversight, or creating a police accountability board with the ability to subpoena an officer when they receive a citizen complaint and the right to depose him or her. Do that, and I believe we'd see a significant decrease in police misconduct.

The biggest obstacle in the way of creating real change in the police state are the police unions. Since police unions came into political power in the 1970s, they have succeeded in shielding their members from public accountability. They forcefully safeguard the rights of members accused of bad behavior, usually through arbitration hearings held behind closed doors. The police unions have also been very effective at holding back much needed and wider change, using their political power and influence to disrupt attempts to increase culpability. Police unions accomplish this by marrying the awesome political power of organized labor supported on the left with a perverse sense of being deserved of respect and reverence without earning it, and in some cases in direct contradiction to their actions. This broad power unites political ideologies more often than not in supporting accountability in secret, which is really no accountability at all. This year, Governor Northam and the democratic legislature of Virginia signed a bill, advanced by Democrats and opposed by Republicans, that for the first time permitted the establishment of unions. Virginia is a right-to-work state. Teachers, police, and other public employees are now allowed to create their own unions.

While rates of union membership have dropped by half nationally since the early 1980s, to 10 percent, for a police officer, if you join and follow the rules, you are never going to be able to report on the bad officers because you won't be allowed to talk. In places where unions don't exist, trade organizations often take their place and cobble together the same amount of power and control.

And it's all about control.

For example, the union rules say a police officer can only talk with a union representative present. There's policy on how to effectuate complaints and there's a process by which you cooperate or not with the Internal Affairs Bureau (IAB). IAB is dedicated to preserving integrity and fighting corruption within police departments. Union representatives never want officers talking to IAB. Often, Internal Affairs is more of a coverup machine than it is an unbiased entity. It's always uncomfortable to figure out how much corruption there is in an entity, but especially in the very people who are supposed to be protecting us. Even with the best motives, it usually boils down to self-protection that keeps leadership from holding officers account-able—that and the massive power of the unions, or both.

If you're a police chief or sheriff, how do you take a stance against your officers?

How would those officers ever accept your command?

Think about an officer who actively recognizes the violation of civil rights and looks away. It happens all the time. It's part of the culture. In fact, police officers who don't either work for the Internal Affairs Bureau or they get fired and black-listed by the brass. Interestingly, as a result of the extreme lobbying efforts by police unions, police disciplinary records are public in only twelve states.

The union is required to represent and defend its members, even when they clearly violate their oath of office. Police unions, like all other unions, will stop at nothing to protect the interests of its members, even if means putting their rights over yours. If you are someone who puts a Blue Lives Matter bumper sticker on your car, you're slapping union propaganda on that bumper.

Sadly, it's not about supporting good police officers, it's about hiding bad ones, and therefore making all good officers bad. Derek Chauvin, the now former

Minneapolis police officer who held his knee on George Floyd's neck, had eighteen prior complaints filed against him before he killed Floyd. Privacy regulations set between the police and union contracts make it impossible to know the exact details. Tou Thao, the officer who stood by while Chauvin knelt on Floyd, had six complaints filed with internal affairs.

The union makes it extremely difficult to discipline officers for their actions by protecting those who should have been fired.

One of the extreme measures police unions would take to protect its hundreds of thousands of members from full transparency is lobbying to make recording an on-duty police officer punishable by fifteen years in prison. Jim Pasco, the executive director of the Fraternal Order of Police, the largest police organization in the country, believes it ought to be illegal for someone to record police with their cellphones. And yet, the use of cellphone camera footage has become an absolute game changer in weeding out the bad officers from the good. Footage of encounters between civilians and police often becomes the most important piece of evidence, especially in cases of police abuse.

I don't believe it's enough to simply speak about a problem and reasonably maintain credibility for affecting change. You must take action. If you recognize there is a problem, you must do something about it. That's why I launched a worldwide app called Bad Cop, Good Cop. The app lets users share and view live law enforcement interactions across the United States and around the world. The video livestreams, which means it can't be deleted by police. Viewers can rank both "good" and "bad" cops based on what they see. I plan to offer $10,000 a month in scholarships for the children of the top ten "good cops" on the app. I believe sunlight is the best disinfectant, and that is why I decided to do something about it.

Police officers not being held accountable for their inexcusable behavior—this is what people in America are tired of. The police state has created a beautiful system for themselves, but it's all about to come crashing down. And that's good. It needs to. It's been wrong for a very long time, and it's gotten progressively worse since the 1960s. It's not worse just because we are seeing these acts of brutality more, it's also because the elite police state sees that it's at risk.

And that's what the burning of Precinct Three represented.

When the people of Minneapolis burned their Precinct Three police station, it was a long overdue statement. It was not unlike the "tea party" that spurned a revolution in our original colonies. Andy Stanley, a prominent evangelical pastor from Atlanta, gave a sermon after the Floyd protests in which he said, "It's no longer enough to be non-racist; one must be anti-racist." Maybe we've reached the tipping point of violence against black citizens. One thing is certain: the corruption and hypocrisy needs to stop.

But it probably won't.

Perhaps, for the first time, the burning of Precinct Three showed weakness on the part of the police. But it also showed something much bigger: it highlighted the people taking power and control over the police. Yes, there was genuine fear for the loss of order and civil society or the possibility it would lead to that. But it also showed that police don't have unlimited power. Only the people do.

The ultimate right of the people in America to overtake those in power is still real, if not for what the Constitution says, but for the sheer determination and grit of the American people. In a time of crisis, the decision was made by the citizens of Minneapolis to overtake that police department. When they did, the police abandoned the station.

That was a watershed moment, one that is very symbolic of the police state in the United States finally stepping back, retreating, and heading down the road to much-needed change.

Not that we should celebrate or admire anyone taking property that isn't theirs. But we have to recognize that sometimes when you are punched, you have to punch back, and that's exactly what some of the people in Minneapolis did.

When the Supreme Court established the doctrine of qualified immunity, it assured us that it would not be a license for lawless conduct for government officials. The Supreme Court was wrong. But if there were to finally be an end to qualified immunity, that would bring power to the people in a way that it has never been given before.

The police learned one thing from the burning of Precinct Three: they learned that if enough people in any one of our cities gathered together, they could take any precinct or police station in this country. I am not suggesting that is what we should do. I am merely pointing out that the police learned this that night. That was a deeply sobering realization for fascists. Are most police officers fascists? No, but most Germans weren't fascist either. You either go along with it, or you don't.

About a week before the killing of Ahmaud Arbery, Jay Pharoah, an actor and comedian best known for his work on *Saturday Night Live,* was jogging in suburban Los Angeles. He was taken down by four gun-wielding police officers in broad daylight. When he asked why the police were doing this, he was told he fit the description of a black man in the area wearing gray shirt and sweatpants. Handcuffed, Pharoah pleaded with the police, saying they had made a mistake, and within minutes, they realized they had. Still, Pharoah had to insist the police Google him before they agreed to remove the handcuffs they had placed around his wrists.

Is this really what it's like for a black man in this country in 2020?

It is.

The thing is, it isn't just black men. *It is all of us.* And it is us versus them. The "them" are organized. They have a union.

As tensions rise, we are seeing more incidents of police misconduct and brutality among all races. What is scary is the reach now goes far beyond the men and women in blue.

Attorney General William Barr unleashed an army of government agents on peaceful demonstrators at Lafayette Square, in Washington, DC. As the president made his way from the White House to St. John's Church, where he infamously held up a Bible for a photo op, these "troops" aggressively pushed protestors out of the way, used tear gas (or pepper spray or some other type of chemical irritant), and used extreme force.

These enforcers were from various government agencies, including:

- the Drug Enforcement Administration
- the FBI
- the Bureau of Alcohol, Tobacco, Firearms and Explosives (ATF)

- the United States Marshals
- the Federal Bureau of Prisons
- Homeland Security
- the Capitol Police
- the Federal Protective Service
- the Secret Service and
- the District of Columbia National Guard

Oddly, the Washington, DC, metropolitan police were not always included in these encounters. Some, like members of the FBI, wore identifying information without names, but most were stripped of personal and agency identification. Protestors had no idea who they were battling.

Utilizing anonymous federal police is not the America we know and love. It certainly creates issues with any type of oversight or accountability of law enforcement who engage in misconduct. And, it's an act of abuse, that, according to the Justice Department in 2014, "conveys a message to community members that through anonymity, officers may seek to act with impunity." We have a right to know who is doing the policing in America.

Deploying active United States troops against Americans is absolutely terrifying. The imagery of federal troops guarding our nation's capital was vivid. It certainly sent the intended message of domination. But it also sent one of tyranny. Without evidence, Attorney General Barr went so far as to suggest that foreign powers may have been using the cover of protests to advance their own agendas against the United States, focusing only on far-left anarchists and completely ignoring arrests of the far-right groups.

As a result of these acts of intimidation and control, our government created new fears well beyond the street violence. Fears about the government itself. If this doesn't set up a feeling of distrust with our government, then I don't know what does.

After they were tear-gassed to clear the way for an administration photo op, some of those DC protestors filed lawsuits through the ACLU—in conjunction with the Washington Lawyers' Committee for Civil Rights and Urban Affairs, the

11

THE POLICE-STATE CHOKEHOLD ON THE FIRST AMENDMENT

WHERE WERE YOU FOR THE FIRST THREE MONTHS OF THE PANDEMIC IN America?

Did you go to work?

Did you eat out?

Did you see your friends?

Did you go to church?

The likelihood is if you quarantined or sheltered at home, your answers are all no, you didn't do any of those things. Like most Americans, you adhered to the government's orders. As a result, many of you lost your jobs and your income, perhaps you weren't able to feed your family or see your loved ones. Even worse, you couldn't be with a loved one if they fell ill.

Extraordinary times require extraordinary circumstances—and, no doubt, the pandemic was a once-in-a-generation occurrence. In economics, the phrase "negative externalities" refers to what happens when production or consumption requires that additional costs outside of the intended use are passed onto the consumer or other third parties and no remuneration is made. Some examples of this include what happens when smokers ignore the harmful effects of cigarettes, the results of the disposal of food waste, and the impact of pollution on our lungs.

If I am speeding on the highway, there is little you can do to stop my reckless choice. When a liberty interest directly and negatively impacts the liberty of another, that too is a negative externality.

Some people may say critical times call for critical and more *controlling* measures. However, if you can accomplish the same impact from providing support, services, and information as you can from providing a heavy-handed direction or control, why wouldn't you? Instead of just being told what to do, people would be happier and more vested in the solution because they're a part of it.

If you are a parent, you certainly understand this process. If you tell your child what to do and don't provide context and understanding, the likelihood is that child isn't going to do what you say. And, he or she certainly won't respect you. If, however, you explain why it's necessary, you likely will get cooperation. If your children are going to do something really dangerous and you don't get them to buy in to your request, well, then it's time say no—but only as a function to protect, not punish.

As free adults, we have the right to make fundamental decisions about how we live our lives. And that right is more powerful than any restriction that government can place on us. Having the choice is what makes us different. During the pandemic, we should have had the choice to wear a mask, or not; go to the store, or not; go to church, or not. These are our choices. There is a difference between *allowing* and *requiring* us to do something.

Calling for the reopening of America would have made more sense to me if the president, the government, and his team of experts had coordinated an effective strategy based on science and expertise out of the gate. Of course, I would have preferred no shutdown at all or at least making decisions that didn't usher in another Great Depression. But if you're going to make a bad decision, at least have a plan for what happens when something goes wrong. But they didn't and, much like the government did during Hurricane Katrina, they failed in the handling of COVID at our expense. I believe the shutdowns could have been avoided. I also believe that leadership starts by setting the example you want others to follow. When the president and vice president refuse to wear masks or openly refute the experts they've brought in to guide the nation through these difficult times, what message is that sending to us?

It makes us wonder, "What's the real story here? What is really behind the shutdown they're blaming on COVID-19 if we are just going to reopen while the virus is still ravaging our communities? And how did we let this get so far out of our control?"

We should have focused on the most at-risk people first. We should never have shut down our economy.

We should have instituted mass testing early on.

We should have been cranking up production of PPE sooner.

We should have been looking at and making decisions centrally, not nationally.

We should have been limiting the federal government's role to invoking the use of the Defense Production Act instead of shipping much-needed supplies to foreign countries.

And most of all, we should *not* have been stripping away our constitutional rights in the process.

I'm a big believer that education and resources are always a better solution than mandating. With education, the American people can make good choices. When we send legislators to state government or to Congress to represent our interests, we know how to get it done because we've done it before and we know what to expect. There is a function by which the American people control the government, not the other way around.

We hold our government accountable. We are not ruled by our government.

I think we can all agree that there are times when the government must curtail individual freedoms to protect the public. But to preserve our rights, those measure have to end when the threat passes.

Think about it like this: There are speed limits on the highway. They aren't temporary, but they are often debated. The legislature has hearings, and people like us can go to those hearings and have a chance to have our voices heard. Sometimes it's experts from the insurance industry who weigh in; other times, it's a representative from the neighborhood watch setting limitations on what we do.

But it all happens in public. Those choices should come from us getting together and deciding that changing the speed limit is a good thing to do. *That* is representative democracy. And that's why we license people to drive, ask them not to drive recklessly, and restrict drinking and driving.

There are going to be restrictions of liberty that any free society is going to have to maintain, but those restrictions should be limited to instances where they protect the liberty interest of another. And those limitations should always rise or fall at the will of a free people, not its government.

The battle between liberty and health in the United States isn't a new one but it has likely never been as extreme in our lifetime as what we are experiencing now. Since the Colonial era, Americans have demanded health during times of crisis and freedom whenever things are status quo.

Not surprisingly, our government has always found ways to manipulate the citizens of the United States by creating extreme tension during those times.

Quarantines and the struggle for liberty in America date back as far as 1701, when members of the Massachusetts Bay Colony waged a battle over the first quarantine laws. They opposed a nationwide quarantine, saying it was too restrictive. During the Spanish flu of 1918, the mayor of Pittsburgh halted all public gatherings in advance of the upcoming election. And, of course, in 2020, the same friction has reared its head in worse ways than we could have ever imagined.

The strategy is to silence the people. Why? If you can silence them, they are a lot easier to control.

When a law student studies the Constitution, one of the first issues discussed on the First Amendment is the concept of screaming "fire" in a crowded theater and why certain speech has to be restricted to protect the public good. That is the foundation of understanding the entire body of law around the First Amendment in the United States.

We need to think about what restrictions on speech mean to a larger community. If you put people at risk, should your speech then be limited? We need to come back to the top of the mountain. Freedom of speech is enshrined in the Constitution. A person should be able to say whatever they want and expect to be judged based on what they say. People who say things that are dangerous, improper, evil, or wrong will be known by their words. Ignorance is not bliss. It's far better to know what people think and encourage them to say it.

Why are we afraid to let people be who they are and why do we force them to edit what they have to say? We've got to go back to a liberty principle around freedom of speech and then understand that part of being at liberty is being uncomfortable. That discomfort means we may also have to tolerate voices we don't like on all sides. However, if, from time to time we are able to listen to what those voices are conveying, perhaps we'll all get a little closer in our beliefs. At the very least, we will know who our neighbors are because we've given people the ability to be themselves.

That's what free people should be able to do. They ought to be able to speak openly and talk among themselves and their community so we can grow together. Of course, that shouldn't negate a free person's right to litigate against someone who slanders them, but the legal issue belongs between people, not between a "free person" and their government.

When we start placing restrictions on speech, people can be jailed and publicly lambasted for their viewpoint. That's a very dangerous place to live as a freedom-loving, patriotic American.

When the Benghazi attacks occurred, at first Hillary Clinton said that the attacks were caused by a video that had been produced mocking Islam. In order to sidestep her responsibility as Secretary of State, Clinton decided to go after the free speech rights of a private person. It was total deflection, and the Secretary knew it. During the Benghazi hearings, Republicans were correct in calling her out. Her defense was to attack the First Amendment to abdicate her responsibility, which was wrong.

One of the greatest examples of the government using its power to restrict speech revolves around the demonization of Linda Tripp for speaking her truth. In many ways, Linda Tripp was a patriot because she spoke up, whether we liked what she was saying or not. It didn't matter that Monica Lewinsky shared certain information or whether you or I would have done what Linda Tripp did. She felt it was her obligation and had every right to speak about what she knew. Once she did, her actions were harshly criticized by political operatives who were trying to protect the president. A large amount of energy was spent trying to make Tripp look horrible when, in fact, President Clinton was in the wrong for his actions. We all witnessed a private citizen speaking out and being attacked by the most powerful government in the world so that the leader of that government could protect himself from being exposed for his own elicit behavior. Clinton's attacks on Monica Lewinsky, Jennifer Flowers, Paula Jones, and Kathleen Willey, just some of the women who alleged that he had sexual impropriety with them, was nothing but a privileged attempt to silence and shut down those people's right to free speech.

Bill Clinton was certainly not the only president with this flaw. We've had many, including Trump, an obvious example. However, we've had many more. Dwight D. Eisenhower, Warren G. Harding, Woodrow Wilson, James Garfield, George H.W. Bush, Lyndon B. Johnson, Grover Cleveland, George Washington, James Buchanan, John F. Kennedy, and Franklin Roosevelt, just to name a few. Finding comfort in the arms of someone other than your spouse isn't something I really care about. But when the government uses its power to silence people to protect the personal interests of a president, we should all pay very close attention. That is *certainly* something I care very much about.

We have to protect the First Amendment in individual assaults to freedom of speech. If we protect it there, we won't worry about it getting to a place where it shuts down whole groups of speech, like we saw during the Ohio riots in the 1960s or the Chicago riots, or anytime free speech events were canceled. People like Candace Owens, an American conservative activist, who was initially critical of Trump and the Republican party, shouldn't be blocked from going to a college campus just because she has become a Trump supporter and a critic of the Democrats. If we let it happen to one or a few, we let it happen to us all.

This is the ultimate hypocrisy of democracy.

People have an absolute right to free speech, not an absolute right to be heard. That is a very different thing. No one in America is obligated to listen to you. But you do have a right to speak. We live in a society that wants everything to feel good. Sometimes, democracy doesn't feel good because there are always going to be winners and losers. Some people are right, which makes some people wrong. We have to respect individual liberty to protect everybody in the process, to clear the way to say, think, and believe what they want. Society works by majority rule and the courts and systems are there to protect individual liberty against mob rule. This system was designed to be simple, by some very smart people who warned us that we could ruin it if we weren't careful. To guide us, they gave us a lot of perennial documents around the founding of our country that tell us what to do. And yet, we fail to treasure what we have.

The right to free speech, assembly, and religion are central to our existence and guaranteed in the First Amendment, yet each were greatly infringed upon during the pandemic. Freedom of speech and assembly really go hand in hand, as it's hard to have one without the other. The founders accumulated those liberties together because they knew that they were inextricably linked. The public square was the place where free speech occurred. Of course, our public square looks dramatically different today from what our founders imagined.

We have so many more resources than our founders did. Our platforms for speech are infinite, and yet we are less effective in controlling the day to day operations of our government.

The government has made numerous attempts to control that speech and assembly. If the government can control who speaks, then it controls who you can listen to. In the process, they can completely control the narrative.

Restricting speech is dangerous, but sometimes it can be misunderstood. If I am having a private event where I have rented the space and it is otherwise under my control, and I choose to throw someone out of that event for saying something I don't like or agree with, I can do that. If I am the president of the United States or a public official, it's a little different. I cannot shut down protestors, but I can halt someone from actively stopping my speech. Protestors have a right to be outside of the venue. If someone comes inside to a private space, they can be removed.

The bigger question is: why are you shutting down public speech?

Why are some people so afraid of an opposing point of view?

The moral of this story is simple. When the government starts restricting speech, it's all about control. And here's one way they do that.

The government makes investments in media all the time. Are we to expect that those investments don't come with expectations? Have you ever made an investment in something where you didn't expect to get something out of it? What you don't expect is to get a quid pro quo of some kind. Do we honestly believe that the government feels the same way?

That is why we have to look at government money in media as an extreme threat to the First Amendment, liberty interests, and particularly free speech. It isn't just about controlling speech. It's about controlling access to speech in a world dominated by digital media.

Digital media has become the modern public square, the place where we get into arguments about access and laws, candidates, and issues. Everyone should have the right to enter the public square and have their say. We can choose to listen, or not.

To some, civil liberties may not feel like a priority during a crisis, but especially during a health catastrophe where hundreds of thousands of Americans are dying from a disease with no vaccine, it ought to be a big priority. Emergency responses should be short term, though, because it's so enticing for the government to use disasters as a gateway to misuse and abuse power that can easily become a part of our daily lives long after the threat has passed.

During the pandemic, some states were more restrictive than others. Some prohibited gatherings where the virus could quickly spread, including all places of worship, while others exempted religious services from their ban. As I mentioned earlier in the book, during the pandemic, I felt very strongly that the parishioners of my church should have a place to gather and share faith. We held a religious service on May 10, 2020, despite Governor Northam's executive orders against gatherings. The Harrisonburg Police Department graciously stood down from citing us for the service, even though local law enforcement agencies held the authority to cite people for violations of Executive Order 53, which closed many businesses and facilities, including churches, and limited gatherings to ten people in Virginia. Most houses of worship did not defy the orders in their states and didn't reopen until the state said they could.

The Supreme Court has said that, "Any infringement on speech or religion must be incidental to the central goal of the restriction," which in this case, was stopping the spread of the coronavirus. But here's the thing: As I wrote these words, the coronavirus was still spreading. Americans were still dying. And we were still being told we needed to cower and hide, but there was no solution in this cowardice.

We will never overcome something we are afraid to face. And if we are afraid to hear others speak, we will never face and overcome this disaster. Speech and assembly are concrete rights ... regardless of the "central goal of the restriction." Stay-at-home orders aren't just unconstitutional; they are un-American. We don't need fearmongering; we need solutions. We don't need to hide under our beds.

We need American exceptionalism.

How does this impact us as some states lift restrictions on their own? What if some states decide to reinstate those same bans days before voting? Would it be politically motivated or for our health and wellbeing? It would be hard to know the difference.

This is the grave danger in restricting our First Amendment rights, especially in times of crisis.

Another time our right to assembly was shut down was in the wake of Hurricane Katrina, although that was regional. This was done in an effort to keep people from gathering in a public health crisis and potentially spreading disease or being injured. The government in Louisiana and New Orleans, especially Mayor Ray Nagin, didn't want people to know how badly the city had failed in the preparation for the initial response to the hurricane. Later developments would indicate that the mayor was drunk on power, corrupt, and abused his position. It was all about shutting people up. Power and no ethics are a deadly combination.

There's no doubt, Hurricane Camille sounded a warning sign in 1969. After a near miss, the city should have done more to prepare New Orleans for a hurricane of this magnitude. The city was trying to keep people from gathering and speaking, especially as they were shutting down. Those in charge went so far as to arrest people who attempted to expose what was happening in the city. People were dying and the police abuses were extreme. They didn't want any exposure or culpability for their poor decisions. Police were hurting, shooting, and, in many cases, killing people. There were countless deaths that were unsolved and uninvestigated related to police involved in shootings and incidences of looting after Katrina hit. At every level of city government, there was a decision to obfuscate and protect themselves. The failures of the city were so purposeful, that those who were involved would eventually go to federal prison. And they should have.

Whenever you give government power over you, the government will use that power to protect itself.

There is a "We don't want you to see what's happening" mentality, or what I refer to as "sleight of hand" because the government distracts from the issue at hand to serve their interests and needs over ours. They want us to look at this bright and shiny thing over here to avoid seeing the real issue over there. We are experiencing this every single day.

In New Orleans, I believe to hide their mistakes and corruption, the state and local government fought FEMA from coming in to help. In some ways, President Bush took it on the chin for the failures of the state and local handling of the hurricane. Notably, eight years later, former Mayor Nagin was prosecuted, convicted, and sentenced to ten years in prison for corruption charges. There is a small ray of sunlight from that outcome, but no offset of the 1,833 people who died as a result of the government's failure.

That, by the way, is how our government keeps getting away with the con.

How much do we lose from being prohibited and held back from telling the truth about the horrors of events such as Hurricane Katrina and the coronavirus? Allowing us our unabridged, God-given rights to speak and gather is the solution to assuring these atrocities never happen again.

There will always be unexpected crises. But we must not lose perspective and the opportunity to grow from these types of challenges.

12

DANGEROUS PRECEDENTS

ACCORDING TO JAMES MADISON, THE SECOND AMENDMENT GIVES US the right to repel the government, which he wrote in Federalist Paper #46. I believe that the 2020 American Revolution has begun. The question is, have we become a dictatorial socialist structured system? Remember when Cubans revolted against Batista? A new American revolution could take us in that socialist direction, or it could revert us back to an individual liberty principle, which means a lot of people are going to have to deal with things they don't like.

Individual liberty means we make commitments to ourselves, our family, and the people that we care about, and then we honor those commitments. After that, we make larger commitments to community, state, and country. Over the course of our nation's history, we lost that kind of system and replaced it with one that's top down, which means a system of control, not individual liberty.

There are those in power who are in power for power's sake—it's the most important thing to them. So those who control this government and the policies of this government and have inflamed tensions between groups to exploit that ability to continue to maintain control, power, and money are the ruling class of America.

Whether you know it or not, we have a ruling class in this country. In fact, it's exactly what George Washington rejected.

What do you think George Washington would think of the Bush family dynasty or the Cuomo, Kennedy, or Clinton political trajectories? He would likely be horrified at the idea that a single family would control that much of the American government.

And he'd be right.

It's America's monarchy. And, it's modern-day imperialism.

It's an "I have, you don't, I'll keep, you won't get" mentality. That's the great modern governing philosophy of the American government.

After the terrorist attacks of September 11, we immediately saw the best of the country rallying behind the people and uniting around their patriotism that we hadn't seen for a long time. It was very inspiring to see people help one another under unimaginable circumstances. But there was also a move, particularly in the executive administration, to use the attacks as an opportunity to secure additional powers. The people who made this decision really thought that the powers would be helpful—necessary even. These decisions are typically made with the best intentions. But remember, even the worst decisions that affect people are often made with the best intentions. The US Patriot Act was an example of that. Scores of people were abused under it, and most of us never realized the extent.

Ashcroft v. Iqbal is a case that was heard in the United States Supreme Court.[16] The Court maintained that leading government officials were not liable for the actions of their underlings without proof that they ordered the purportedly biased action. If you are going to sue the government, you have to plead, with specificity, your claims.

In November 2001, Javaid Iqbal, a Pakistani-American from Hicksville, New York, was arrested on charges of conspiracy to defraud the United States and fraud in relation to identification documents. He was arrested by the NYPD and taken into custody. He was placed in a pretrial detention center in Brooklyn. Iqbal alleged the FBI officials carried out a discriminatory policy by designating him a person of high interest in the investigation of the September 11 attacks solely based on his race, religion, and national origin—basically he was taken into federal custody because he was a Muslim man. He was placed in a maximum-security special-housing unit for six months while he was awaiting his fraud trial. Iqbal claimed prison guards brutally beat him, punching him in the face and stomach and dragging him across the room. After being attacked a second time, he sought medical attention, but was denied care for two weeks. The prison guards subjected him to unjustified body cavity searches, called him a terrorist and a "Muslim killer," refused to provide him with adequate food, and intentionally turned on the air conditioning in the winter and the heat in the summer. He also claimed the prison guards interfered with his attempts to pray and engage in religious study, and they denied him access to counsel.

No one in the government has ever refuted that any of these happened. The question was whether or not the government could be held accountable.

Iqbal pleaded guilty to using another man's Social Security card on April 22, 2002. He served prison time until his release on January 15, 2003, and was later deported to Pakistan. After his release, Iqbal brought claims under implied causes of action for violations of his First, Fourth, Fifth, Sixth, and Eighth Amendment rights, as well as other various statutory claims seeking compensatory and punitive damages. Iqbal argued that then-FBI Director Robert Mueller and former United States Attorney General John Ashcroft personally gave the orders and condoned the decision to detain him as well as other Arab immigrants to the United States.

At issue was whether current and former federal officials, including Robert Mueller and John Ashcroft, were entitled to qualified immunity against an allegation that they knew of or condoned racial and religious discrimination against individuals detained after the September 11 attacks. The federal government argued that Iqbal's legal filings were not specific enough to link the government officials with a policy of detaining Arab immigrants and Muslims.

There's no way to plead with specificity without getting discovery in a lawsuit. That's what discovery is for.

So, what the court did was preclude the claim. It's called a "heightened pleading standard." If I want to sue you for breach of contract, I can drop a few lines on a pleading, file it, and it's done. If I want to sue you for fraud, there's something called a heightened pleading standard, because the notion of fraud carries such a negative connotation and is a serious allegation.

The Iqbal standard perverts that protection of the American people in the legal venue and instead protects the government. Any suit against the government must adhere to a heightened pleading standard. The Supreme Court held that

Iqbal's complaint failed to plead sufficient facts to state a claim for purposeful and unlawful discrimination.

While we did disrupt other attacks after September 11, imagine if we had placed as much energy on disrupting them *before*. When governments fail, especially after they miss something they actually had responsibility for, such as national security, they often respond in the extreme by taking away rights and liberties as part of the solution. How does that make any sense? The government failed and we pay for it? This decision to take away more rights and liberties is always a reactionary result from a government's own failure after being caught being corrupt or abusive of its power. The government doesn't believe it needs to respect the liberty interest of a free people. It believes that if it takes more of our liberty interest away, it will be easier to control us.

We see this every day in government, in the way police are interacting, especially in the wake of the heightened civil unrest in the country during the spring and summer of 2020.

Ashcroft v. Iqbal also set a dangerous precedence in law. The Patriot Act was the vehicle for federal agents to begin interrogating Iqbal because they believed he was of Muslim descent. The same could be said about the people who were arrested, taken out of the country, and ended up in Guantanamo Bay or Abu Ghraib. There are significant and well documented abuses related to enhanced interrogation— aka, torture. All of those scars came out of the United States Patriot Act and our government's response to the terrorist attacks of September 11.

Another example of how the government uses crisis to gain more power and control over us is when the feds put together TARP funding to save the banks that had engaged in risky lending practices in 2008. The Troubled Asset Relief Program (TARP) is a program the United States government established by Congress and signed by President George W. Bush to buy distressed assets and equity from banks to strengthen the financial sector after the economic crisis.

The goal was to create several programs that would help stabilize the housing and mortgage industry, as well as the economy, to restart the financial system that was, at the time, extremely distressed. Failing to do so would have resulted in countless foreclosures, leaving those families homeless. Even banks that did not engage in risky lending practices or in the mortgage industry were forced to take those loans and grants.

The government already had intense regulation on banks, which is a good thing. We want our money to be protected. But if there are additional protections necessary under the FDIC program, then there are appropriate ways to request those additional powers other than a power grab during a national financial crisis.

The result of TARP was incredibly increased government regulation into the daily operations of those banks. The power grab gave the government control over an entire sector of the banking industry, which made a lot of people very rich.

None of us, of course.

Many Americans were on the brink of financial disaster, struggling and worrying whether we'd be able to keep our homes. There wasn't a big bank in the industry that didn't have their hands dirty or take a bailout from all of us.

And what did we get for it? Harder, more difficult banking relationships, more difficult access to credit, and certainly challenges in buying or refinancing a home.

The American people got the short end of the stick as a direct result of the TARP funding.

In 2008, Congress originally approved $700 billion for TARP; that authorization was lowered to $475 billion by the Dodd-Frank Wall Street Reform and Consumer Protection Act (Dodd-Frank Act). The authority to make new financial commitments under TARP ended on October 3, 2010. As of October 31, 2016, cumulative collections under TARP, together with Treasury's additional proceeds from the sale of non-TARP shares of AIG, exceeded total disbursements by more than $7.9 billion. Treasury is now winding down its remaining TARP investments and is also continuing to implement TARP initiatives to help struggling homeowners avoid foreclosure.

Anything that binds you into a relationship with the government is a con. You do not need the government to live and be a free person. We resolved that when we recognized our unalienable rights, endowed by a Creator. The government needs to control you to have power. The government's decision to offer banks a bailout in 2008 was really a function to gain control; a large stimulus offer usually is. We certainly have seen the government do the same during COVID-19, where we have seen huge investments in small businesses.

What we won't know for a long time are the long-term ramifications of their actions. I suspect they will be significant and, once again, you and I will pay the very high price for the government's knee-jerk decision-making during a crisis. We have created generational disturbances to significant economic sectors like our retail and food service industries, and these industries will bleed jobs when government assistance winds down. When that happens, I shudder to think about the fallout. You can expect unemployment, bread lines, and poverty levels in record numbers.

It's been a very long time since we've allowed ourselves to believe that we need the level of control we are accepting from the government. They are very happy to take it and equally hesitant to give it back. Every day I feel as though we are losing precious things. The government knows that the single greatest function of control it has isn't its police states, although it uses that well. It isn't the courts, although it uses that well too. It's money. And if you can print money and have people believe it doesn't matter, then you become the most powerful entity in the world—that is, until it all collapses. And, it's the collapse I hope we can avoid.

It's really hard to imagine we'll soft-land this post-COVID economic and civil unrest crisis. If we do, it will be around an understanding that the only thing that protects us from the government is our constitutional rights. There has to be some kind of a revival in the country related to individual liberty. If we can get there, the pain that we go through will likely be cathartic and will hopefully advance us to a better place. If we don't, the new not free America will represent a lasting legacy of our generation as being the first to hand their kids a collection of third world states and or countries. America survived its great Civil War through amazing leadership, but we don't have an identifiable Lincoln of our time yet.

The American people cannot and should not await a leader to inspire our liberty interest.

We must unite together now to join in a shared commitment, a pledge to liberty, to save our country and the future for our children.

13

THINK IT CAN'T HAPPEN HERE? THINK AGAIN!

THOMAS JEFFERSON BELIEVED THE GREATEST WEAPON THE PEOPLE HAD against government was fear. He argued that the government would respect liberty only if it feared losing power.

If we are honest about where we are as a country, the picture is really grim. If we don't take control of our nation, we are possibly only six months to a year away from not being able to feed our families and potentially one to three years away from a militarized revolution.

The real risk of COVID-19 was never the virus and its death toll. Once the virus spread, our government knew many people would get sick and that some would die. They also knew there was no way to put the genie back in the bottle. However, the decisions that were made have created policies that created great risk for all of us.

Let me be clear and brutally candid with you: We may very well be the American generation that witnesses several successive catastrophes, including a mass economic collapse, a banking collapse, radical increases in state power that dramatically eliminate personal liberty, forced vaccines, and even civil war. If we go there, we should know that a civil war in the 2020s will look very different than the Civil War, our first internal secession-induced military conflict. The next civil war will look more like terrorism in our neighborhoods, where you can't go to the store or send your kids to school without knowing they may not come back.

We are talking about America under siege and at war in every community at varying levels. There will be wars focused on race and class and not only a war that puts our liberty to the test, but a war that could place liberty across our nation and indeed the globe in crisis. Think about it. This great nation began as thirteen little colonies. It isn't hard to imagine that the radical little colonies that inspired freedom around the world may just as easily extinguish that flame by not being good stewards of our founders' promise. We are quite simply living in a time of culmination, a time where we will realize the promise of America or be crushed under the weight of the hypocrisy of that promise in practice.

It is a choice, and that choice is ours.

Outside of wartime, we've never had a federal government take as much power as this federal government, but we've also never had the state governments take the kind of power we witnessed during the pandemic. With the widespread civil rights abuses we have endured across the nation in response to the COVID-19 pandemic, it is not surprising to see citizens taking a stand and demanding their rights not be violated. The America we knew and loved before the pandemic has changed, perhaps forever. The mishandling of the virus, the lack of response, and all of the attention that has focused on government control over education and support, has forever shifted the direction of this county.

Americans being told to stay in their homes, being placed on mandatory lockdowns, and in some places threatened with jail if they violate those orders is not *my* America. And it's surely not freedom.

What are you willing to sacrifice to create change and to feel safe? And, what would you be willing to tolerate to keep things exactly as they are? People who have things want to keep them. And if you have enough things, then the risk of losing it can be so bad that you're willing to do horrible things to keep them. And that is true with the American elite.

We are living through the biggest expansion of government authority in generations. Outside of wartime, this kind of government power and control over its citizens in the United States has never happened. And the American people seem to have fallen behind the consensus that we need to "do more" or abdicate more liberty.

When it comes to our government, we are accepting abject failure. Our governments—our federal, state, and local governments—have failed us. Not once or twice, not just recently, but for centuries.

I care about my well-being and that of my family far more than any bureaucrat in Richmond or Washington, DC, ever will. And that means that if I am responsible for keeping my family safe, I am going to do more to keep them safe than the government does. But guess what? Even if you are on your own, even if you have no family or very little family, even if you have no friends, the people you do have in your life still care more about you than your government does. And that was the whole point of the American revolution—the idea that people mattered before governments so much that a government could be of, by, and for those people.

When the president of the United States failed at leading us through the pandemic, New York Governor Andrew Cuomo became the voice of the people. And the leaders of his surrounding states, including New Jersey, Connecticut, and Pennsylvania, did as well. That alliance should have alarmed us all. No governor should have a say in how any other state functions. And we saw California's governor, Gavin Newsom, who runs the third largest economy in the world, function as if California had already seceded from the union, something that has been talked about for many years.

Historically, people who acquire a large amount of power typically don't want to give it away so fast.

This begs the question: What do we do with the monsters we've created?

The idea of people managing people and our own affairs could work in some sort of complex tapestry of watching the better angels of ourselves come into existence. Our history hasn't been perfect because our country is scarred and marred with horrible biases and terrors we've committed. There's no doubt there are moments of shame for actions of our past, yet we can be proud of American redemption and advancement and for the lessons learned because of it, especially our ever-alive search and quest for knowledge that forces us to tear down barriers and overcome biases.

Because of the coronavirus, and because our government wasn't properly prepared, a propaganda machine emerged that has grown much larger in size and in severity as a problem than the virus itself. Abdicating civil liberties to allow big government to become even bigger makes no sense. We also allowed private industry to get bigger too. Google and Apple combined resources to provide contact tracing to over three billion people. They were able to add technology to their smartphone platforms that allow users to be alerted if they come into contact with a person who has COVID-19.

During the pandemic, police in Florida were aggregating information about its citizens test results for the coronavirus so that law enforcement could track people who have the disease or who had symptoms of the disease.

On the surface, that makes sense: government needs to know who is sick, who is not.

But what happens if you don't report? What does the government plan to do with that list?

And how did Florida's unconstitutional personal-data aggregation help them overcome the virus? If you're going to violate our civil liberties, shouldn't we get something in return? The people of Florida have been horribly failed throughout the pandemic from preparedness to testing. So what good were those lists to the residents of that state?

Police lists of people who test positive or who may have had symptoms of the coronavirus is the first step leading to what we saw in Wuhan, when the Chinese police entered homes and dragged people out. We're giving the government too much power, power that comes with consequences as the fears grow and the very difficult rules of bureaucracy and control are implemented.

While this might seem like a good idea to keep you safe, it is also a blatant violation of privacy. Where does that information go and how will it be used? World history is a pretty good indicator that it rarely ends well. The government tracking this type of information and having private companies do it—companies we couldn't possibly divorce ourselves from even if we wanted to—is more dangerous than the disease.

Early on, Dr. Anthony Fauci openly talked about the possibility that we, as Americans, could eventually have to carry certificates of immunity to the coronavirus. Now, international travel requires such certificates, and it's reasonable to expect domestic travel will follow suit. Do you want to have to carry around papers that say you're "safe"? Will people with this government paper be allowed to move and people that don't have the paper won't be? In Revelation 13:16–17, John writes "And he causeth all, both small and great, rich and poor, free and bond, to receive a mark in their right hand, or in their foreheads: And that no man might buy or sell, save he that had the mark, or the name of the beast, or the number of his name." I could never have imagined that such a scriptural reference, which always seemed so bizarre to me in concept, could actually be coming to pass in my lifetime.

There has been a fundamental change in our government and your interaction with it, especially the persecution of people of color, socioeconomically disadvantaged white people, and anyone who doesn't have enough money to make noise to matter in a room full of white millionaires.

That is not the country that our forefathers established, and it isn't the country that was promised to us. And now, we are on a cliff, one that is of our own creating. We have the ability to choose whether we jump or go in another direction with a very big disparity in difference of the result.

What kind of America do *you* want?

On February 20, 1905, the Supreme Court ruled on the case *Jacobson v. Massachusetts,* stating that, "the city of Cambridge, Massachusetts, could fine residents who refused to receive smallpox injections."[17] In 1901, a smallpox outbreak was infiltrating areas across the Northeast. As a result, the state of Massachusetts and the city of Cambridge required all adults to receive a smallpox vaccine. Anyone who refused, was subject to a five-dollar fine.

In 1902, Pastor Henning Jacobson, claimed he and his son both were injured by previous vaccines they had received in Sweden, and therefore refused to be vaccinated. They were more than willing to pay the fine. The city and state prosecuted Jacobson for his rebuff to be inoculated. During his trial, Jacobson argued the vaccine law violated the Massachusetts and federal constitutions. However, the state courts, including the Massachusetts Supreme Judicial Court, rejected his claims. Jacobson had argued that a "compulsion to introduce disease into a healthy system is a violation of liberty."[18]

Three years later, on February 20, 1905, the United States Supreme Court rejected Jacobson's argument. Jacobson had argued that the Massachusetts law requiring mandatory vaccination was a violation of due process under the Fourteenth Amendment, In their response, Justice John Marshall Harlan wrote about the police power of states to regulate for the protection of public health: "The good and welfare of the Commonwealth, of which the legislature is primarily the judge, is the basis on which the police power rests in Massachusetts," Harlan said "upon the principle of self-defense, of paramount necessity, a community has the right to protect itself against an epidemic of disease which threatens the safety of its members."[19] The Supreme Court said the state has the right to force vaccinate an adult because the public health interest of the state outweighs the individual liberty interest.

Essentially, the court said individual liberty isn't possible when it comes to vaccines.

This decision was ultimately a function of control. Nobody really cared if Jacobson himself got the smallpox vaccine or not. They needed everyone to take it. Why? To cure a horrible disease. Obviously, the vaccine worked. However, did the ends (which are wonderful) justify the means (the abdication of individual liberty)? I think not.

The question is whether the government gets to tell you what to do in all areas and preserve their power to abdicate liberty interests. The individual interest isn't the issue. It's the government's interest. And if we, the people, are willing to abdicate that interest, we will never be free again.

However, liberty requires something from all of us. It's hard, but it's worth it. Looking at crises of the past, we haven't always done well coming out of them without substantial long-term effects on our society. An example of this is the Patriot Act enacted after the attacks of 9/11. The idea behind the act is to source potential money-laundering activity. The response of creating the Patriot Act was appropriate. We as a nation were attacked by terrorists who financed those attacks through our own banking system. Before 2002, if you walked into a bank to open an account, it was a ten-minute process. Now it takes a half hour or longer to open a bank account because they have to search databases for your information to see if federal agencies might be interested in you. That happens now every day to everybody that opens a bank account in America. Every single person who engages in commerce related to banking in this country goes on a list run by the Treasury Department.

We always had FISA courts in the United States. FISA courts are secret courts that deal with "issues of national security." These courts were designed to give broad powers to federal prosecutors engaged in combating terrorist operations. They were allowed to use no-knock warrants or no-disturb warrants, which give police officers the right to go through your things without notifying you. They can literally break into your house when you're not there and go through everything. They can catalogue all of your personal belonging, take pictures and videos, and when they're finished violating your privacy, they can leave everything just as they found it. You may have no idea anyone was ever there. What they do afterward is even worse. They take all of the evidence they obtained and construct a case against you. Several weeks later, your house can be surrounded by officers whom will know exactly what to look for and where to find it. There is nothing they won't seek or discover.

A no-knock warrant is scary enough, but a no-disturb warrant is something that should not exist in the United States of America. As long as law enforcement can go to a secret FISA court and get a no-disturb warrant, we are not free.

Prior to the enactment of the Patriot Act, an American was never going to be tried in a FISA court. If you got caught buying marijuana and the feds thought you might be a dealer, FISA courts were never the jurisdiction to handle such crimes. However, the Patriot Act changed that by making it possible for FISA to be used for anything. If they can make a connection, you can now be the subject of a warrant issued by the FISA court. So, now we have a hyped-up FISA court, more secretive than ever. FISA cases are not reviewable. Police can go to those courts and get warrants for you under the Patriot Act, even though you have nothing to do with terrorism, just because there *might* be a connection. And then that FISA court will issues a warrant that allows the feds to go into your home, look around, put everything back, then leave and never tell you they were there. This is unconscionable.

What happened to our right to privacy?

While I am certain there are cases where this type of covert activity and investigation makes sense, I am equally certain this is happening to people who are being investigated for opiate abuse or selling meth, particularly when the source of those drugs can be determined to be from overseas. These are not great things to support, but they are not things that need FISA courts. We have courts of local jurisdiction for such crimes. We have grand juries for that. And even though those processes don't necessarily guarantee liberty, at least some costume character wearing a black robe is going to pretend to consider the constitutional rights of the accused. There is no way a FISA court would do that because no one really knows who they are or what civil liberties they are violating. They are not accountable to anyone. Just ask Carter Page if there is something called the Deep State.

Whether you realize it or not, the Deep State has always existed in America. The Deep State isn't a group of Democratic socialists who are planning on taking over free America. That's what the Republicans and especially the right wing like to think. It isn't the Trump supporters who are hell-bent on destroying America, which is what many liberals think. The real Deep State does its work secretively and without any regrets for it. That has always been the cost of doing business, something we all pay for with our taxes. The real Deep State is the people who have things versus the people who don't have things—and the people who have things will always want to keep those things. Human destiny has always been sabotaged by those who seek and gain power over others. People who acquire power hire other people to keep others from stealing their power.

The Patriot Act serves no real legitimate purpose and simply exists to complicate the lives of everyday Americans. It was a government power grab. And if you don't think the government is grabbing power, you're not paying attention.

The president of the United States took great powers, wartime powers, Defense Production Act powers to take over companies, and yet we weren't getting enough COVID-19 tests into communities. The federal government sent out brand-new versions of the fifteen-minute COVID test and each state was merely given a small number of testing kits. How were we ever going to solve our testing crisis with one hundred tests per state?

We weren't.

And that was the point.

There was no vaccine, and, as of the writing of this book, there still isn't. Maybe we will see one in the near future, or maybe we won't. But even if we do, will it matter?

And we're not alone here. Other countries around the world used the pandemic as a power grab too. Peru gave its president extensive new legislative clout that practically made him a dictator. It was easy to see that, around the world, governments were using this power for their own purposes.

That's what governments do. And that's what tyrants do.

When the Third Amendment ("No Soldier shall, in time of peace be quartered in any house, without the consent of the Owner, nor in time of war, but in a manner to be prescribed by law") was created, it prevented the military from housing soldiers in our homes. When the Constitution was ratified, accommodating soldiers was a major concern in the colonies. Prior to the Revolution, whenever Britain launched a military attack on our soil, their soldiers still needed housing. This responsibility fell to the American colonies, which meant quartering British soldiers in our private homes.

Ultimately, the founders believed the quartering of troops was a justification for autonomy and, therefore, made it a part of the Declaration of Independence. The Bill of Rights anticipated, in a time when it was feasible to imagine, that American military troops may need to invade the homes of American citizens for quartering. At the time, it was how the troops moved and so it became part of how we anticipated we would have to protect Americans from the possibility that the military would seize whole towns to set up camps. It wasn't like it is today, where we can transport troops to wherever they need to go. It was just a function of where we were in time.

We shouldn't have to worry about that today because we don't quarter soldiers in this country anymore, right?

Not necessarily.

During the pandemic the prospect of a national vaccine movement commanded by the military was and remains a very real possibility. President Trump actually promised we would see military troops across the country, delivering these vaccines directly to our doors.

What happens if you don't open the door and, like Pastor Henning Jacobson, you ultimately refuse the vaccine?

When a soldier is standing in your home, the likelihood is the military will be empowered to detain you.

What rights will you have to challenge a forced vaccine?

Would businesses, such as hotels, be able to deny a squad of soldiers working in their community from staying in their hotel? The answer is no. During the militarization of Washington, DC, following the George Floyd shooting, military troops were quartered at the Park Hyatt hotel. You can be sure that they didn't pay rack rates, and one of Washington, DC's, most iconic boutique hotels was turned into a war zone. A hotel clerk told me that armed soldiers were filling the lobby, wielding large guns, and intimidating guests, and the hotel was helpless to deny them quartering.

If this military does go out to distribute vaccines, this scene will be repeated in every state, city, and town across America.

Personally, I prefer my doctors to wear a mask and not carry a machine gun.

Now, more than ever, we have to look at potential Third Amendment violations, not from the traditional perspective of allowing soldiers in our homes but rather something altogether more ominous: soldiers coming ino our homes to vaccinate us and our families.

What do you say to the man or woman standing in your living room, holding an AK-47 and a syringe?

You and your children get the vaccine.

That's exactly why the president said he would use the military. It's overwhelming force and total domination. Unbelievably, those are the words spoken by the champion of conservatives in the country. And to be certain, you cannot look to the left to defend your constitutional liberties either. Nancy Pelosi and

Chuck Schumer have never met a government program they didn't like. Remember, government programs by their very nature restrict our freedom, quickly become bureaucratic, and are difficult to manage. Pelosi and Schumer only want to insert more government into our lives. They campaign on it.

But at least they're honest about those intentions.

Engblom v. Carey was a 1982 case decided by the United States Court of Appeals for the Second Circuit.[20] It is one of the very few decisions to directly challenge the Third Amendment.

The case was introduced in 1979 after a strike by New York State correction officers. During the strike, some of their duties were performed by National Guardsman, who were called to serve. The strike took place at the Mid-Orange Correctional Facility as well as others around the state. Those employees who went on strike were quickly removed from their state-provided employee housing. When the National Guard arrived, they were housed in those quarters. Two of the evicted officers at Mid-Orange Correctional Facility, Marianne E. Engblom and Charles E. Palmer, later filed a lawsuit against the state of New York and then Governor Hugh Carey.

The decision established three things: one, the court said national guardsmen are soldiers; two, the Third Amendment applies to the state as well as the federal authorities; and three, the Third Amendment extended beyond the homeowners. The first point is important because as state entities, an argument was made that they weren't actually soldiers the way the Constitution intended. The court disagreed. The second portion of the decision demonstrates that the Fourteenth Amendment gives those protections to Americans not just from the federal government, but from state governments as well. The case was remanded to district court, where it was decided in the defendants' favor again, due to the principle that, as agents of the state, the defendants were covered by a qualified immunity unless they were knowingly acting illegally. In the absence of previous precedents on this issue, the standard of "knowing illegality" was not met.

From the time COVID-19 reared its ugly head on our shores and our cities and states were forced into lockdown, hotels were not given that right. By mandate, many were turned into hospitals or places where frontline workers slept or seized in places like Los Angeles and San Diego to house the homeless. While I would never suggest that we displace essential workers or the homeless, nonetheless, for the hotel owner, it's unconstitutional to take over his place of business without his permission. To really drive this point home, a homeless man entered the Ritz-Carlton Hotel in Beverly Hills, California, and refused to leave. He was conscripting the hotel pursuant to Governor Newsom's guidance to house the homeless during the pandemic. This particular Ritz-Carlton has residential floors with apartments some costing upwards of $42 million. The Ritz-Carlton wasn't going to grant this man a stay with open arms. They had him arrested and escorted out of the hotel.

The point is valid though. If we can take over the Travelodge, why can't we do the same with the Ritz-Carlton? The mere fact that the Ritz-Carlton is nicer means nothing if property rights don't matter. This is why the end justifying the means is a very dangerous thing. Whose end and means are we serving?

If you're a homeless person, the end is survival. If you're an elite, and you own a private island and a jet and a helicopter to get you there, you're in power because you have more to lose. And no one wants to imagine losing anything because of a pandemic, especially their life. That's why individual liberty interest matters. The end won't justify the means for the homeless, but it might justify the means for the rich and powerful.

It doesn't work for one person to choose whether the end justifies the means because it won't for everyone. In fact, that's true for most people.

The Fourth Amendment to the Constitution ("The right of the people to be secure in their persons, houses, papers, and effects, against unreasonable searches and seizures, shall not be violated") forbids unreasonable searches and seizures of individuals and property. What we know from the Constitution is that there needs to be a judicial officer involved in the process. Each state has a different process by which that happens. If the police knock on your door and say they're there to search your home, what's the first thing you would say?

"Do you have a warrant?"

Even if they do, they will likely tell you to step aside.

What do you do?

Some of you might respond by saying, "Show me the warrant." And others might just comply.

Now, what if you are an African American?

If you say no or stand up to the police officer, he might put you on the ground.

Here's the thing. The Fourth Amendment is only as good as our ability to hold police accountable. Since we know we can't, the Fourth Amendment is meaningless.

Even if you can prove the police violated your Fourth Amendment rights, qualified immunity says you can't sue them. There would never be a court case and, therefore, there would never be justice. When Randy Weaver didn't want to let the police inside his home, they slaughtered his family. The only time the Fourth Amendment matters any more is in criminal cases where people had something they weren't supposed to have and got caught.

Even if we were in a place where everyone played by the rules, and we could, for a moment, suspend the idea that there aren't bad police officers who do bad things, the system is still broken. Let's say you get pulled over by the police for a traffic violation. If that police officer says he smelled marijuana (in a state where it is not legal), it is probable cause for him to search your car. That is not what the Constitution envisioned when the founders created the Fourth Amendment. There is no Fourth Amendment right if exercising that right is dependent on the police officer not lying about it. There has to be proof that you've done something wrong before they can search you. The idea that the person lying is a police officer doesn't mean there was proof. There must be actual evidence.

Our law firm represented a case, *Varner v. Roane,* that involved a young man who worked at a hamburger shop.[21] The police come to his place of employment and said, "Come outside. I want to talk to you." This officer worked in narcotics and had been watching our client for some time. He believed Varner had drugs on him or was holding them in his truck. The officer said he wanted to search the vehicle. Varner said no. The officer then threatened to bring the K-9 unit, which he did. The dog arrived, the officer walked around the front of the truck and tapped it three times. At that moment, the dog alerted exactly to that space. It's easy to false alert a dog, and it happens more than you might think. You have to be able to false alert the dog to test a real response. In this case, it seems obvious that was what this officer did. And perhaps because the officer knew he would be covered by qualified immunity, he didn't care that Varner witnessed his false alert. When the dog alerted, the officer had probable cause to search the car. When he did, he found no drugs. While the district court dismissed the case, it remains on appeal and I believe it will be overturned.

We've funded representation for hundreds of cases I feared we couldn't win on illegal search and seizure. I do so to create precedence and help our clients seek the justice they so rightly deserve. One such case was for a client from Georgia named Treneshia Dukes. Treneshia was sleeping in her boyfriend's apartment when the window next to her bed was broken and a grenade was thrown onto her pregnant stomach, killing her baby. The culprits? Police officers executing a no-knock warrant because they observed the potential sale of a small amount of marijuana. No-knock warrants marry some of the worst examples of police abuse we can imagine, allowing officers to invade your home without announcing themselves. They can even hurt and kill you. Sometimes, they can enter the wrong house. Even if they do, it doesn't matter, because police in America have zero accountability. Government breeds inefficiency because it never holds itself accountable. We have to stop that. Otherwise, people like Treneshia will continue to be beaten or burned with no justice to follow.

I want less government in my life.

And, I want less encroachment on the individual liberties of Americans.

During the pandemic, legislation was quietly passed amending the Patriot Act to allow significant unconstitutional surveillance, such as warrantless web searches or access to your phone records. For the most part, Americans were completely unaware that these changes were taking place. Every time the Patriot Act is renewed, our government authorizes requests for additional powers. Those requests are sometimes granted or rejected. Thankfully, the passed legislation was as quietly overturned as it was passed, as it was a bridge too far, even for our government. But the Patriot Act still exists, which means we still allow law enforcement across this country to make application to secret courts, to get no-knock warrants, and, worse, no-disturb warrants.

The conundrum is obvious. If I can't go to the leaders on the left, and I have a president who wants the military in American cities and total domination of the people, what is the alternative? What option is there that meets this important need?

Do you want a government that tells you what to do or do you want a government that you tell what to do?

If you want a government that tells you what to do, keep doing what we're doing. Stay silent. Don't take action. Push the pedal to the metal and enjoy losing every freedom you've ever had. And for some, that might be just fine. Those are the people who live in the middle of the page, those who don't like to make decisions, especially difficult ones that affect great change. I get it. Decisions can be stressful and sometimes it's nice to have someone, anyone, even your government make one for you—that is, until you disagree.

But once you've abdicated your ability to make decisions, it doesn't matter if you disagree or not.

That's the rub of being a free people.

Free people become lazy when they don't have to fight for their freedom. It becomes an expectation. And, if you believe you are free because you live in America, it's time to wake up. The fight is here and if we don't work now to critically and importantly scale back the powers of federal, state, and local governments, we are never going to be a free people again.

The Supreme Court handed down a landmark decision ruling on *Bostock v. Clayton County*, recognizing that federal employment-law protections apply to millions of lesbian, gay, bisexual, and transgender workers.[22] In the same week, the Supreme Court rejected a slew of cases revisiting the controversial legal doctrine of qualified immunity that shields law enforcement and government officials from being sued for actions taken in an official capacity. As a gay man, I couldn't be prouder that the Supreme Court saw its way to recognizing rights for the LGBTQ community. But how can I celebrate that win when their decision to refuse to hear the many cases of police brutality and misconduct that impacts the brown and black communities in our country?

The laws are not supposed to protect some of us. They ought to protect all of us.

And, it's exactly why individual liberty determinations are most important in the United States. If your individual liberty matters as much as mine and we're the arbiter of protecting it, then it's up to you and it's up to me to take care of each other. That was the foundation on which our government was based.

Change needs to come from demands, not just protests in the street. It isn't about BLM, Antifa, the militia movement. It isn't about people like Randy Weaver or the Branch Davidians. It has got to be about *everybody*. All of us who care about being free in this country need to stand up and demand that the abuse of constitutional liberties must come to an end.

The only way we are going to achieve that is if we reject the pitting of American's extremes against one another in an attempt to drive the governments total and complete control. And believe me when I say that they government is doing a really good job of dominating us. If there's ever been a window for Americans to wake up and realize what is happening, it is *now*.

The interest of the right and the left have never been *more* aligned.

Stop and think about that.

COVID-19 exposed the ways and means in which our government has been breaking, bending, and manipulating our rights. The protective sphere of the privilege quotient has burst. After the attacks on 9/11, wealthy Arab-American families would say the privilege bracket left them for a period of time. But their affluence probably got them back in privilege faster than poor Arab men and women, or activist Arabs. And now, the privilege quotient has evaporated for a large number of people on the right. The virus has made them suddenly understand they're not free and that their constitutional liberties mean nothing. The minute those people are affected by the same lack of rights as so many others in our country—the minute they fear losing their power, money, and control—it's a whole new ballgame. Even if the people gathering around the country making their voices heard don't fundamentally agree on their issues, there's no questions they still agree on the very foundational principle of liberty.

That is the only thing that matters.

Standing up and fighting for our rights may be our only option left. That fighting starts in our courts, legislatures, and on our streets. The fighting starts peacefully but rarely ends that way. In order to keep the fight peaceful, you have to be able to establish basic ground rules that protect your rights to make those arguments. And that's exactly what so many people are gathering for. And what we should *all* be demanding.

Liberty for all.

What unites us, Republicans and Democrats, right and left, is that people who have things want to keep those things, especially our freedom. And it's equally true that sometimes people who feel as though they don't have something they desire, feel as if they need to take it from people who have it.

There are a finite number of things in the world. If you have a lot, you're not interested in people exercising their liberty because the liberty interest might give them the right to compete. And if they compete, you might lose. The more you get, the less liberty minded and more protectionist you become. Think about the comment that Governor Cuomo made during one of his press conferences in May 2020. He took to the stage with one of his impressive PowerPoint presentations, showing with great transparency the number of people who died the day before, and he began to talk as he usually did. He posed an important question, one I thought was quite intelligent to ask: "What have we learned from the coronavirus?"

He said:

Government is important again, right? Government, most days you lead your life, government, politics, it's a sideshow. It's not that important. When does government really become important? Probably, almost not in my lifetime. When has it been vital? It's vital at the time of war, crisis, real national crisis. But that's the only time it's really vital. When you don't have a choice but to deal with and rely on government. . . . You have to be competent at what you do. There's something called government and you either know how to do it or you don't know how to do it. You know, for many years, anyone can be in government. You know. I don't know, can anyone be a nurse? Oh no. You have to know what you're talking about. Can anyone be a doctor? No. No. You have to know what you're talking about. Can anyone be a lawyer? No. No. No. No. You have to know what you're talking about. Can anyone be a plumber? Nope. You have to know what you're talking about. Can anyone run government? Oh yeah. Anybody can run government.[23]

Think about that for a second. It is the clearest delineation of what the elites want America to look like. Jefferson once said that as soon as some legislature was critical to the success of the republic, he wanted farmers in the legislature. I believe Andrew Cuomo doesn't want people in the legislature unless they agree with him. If they don't agree with him, if he thinks they're stupid and unqualified, they shouldn't be allowed in the government. Apparently, he doesn't believe that the American people can be trusted with that decision. People have the right to choose whomever they want to be in their government. You may not agree with who wins, but it's the people's choice!

The danger that we could lose everything is very real. Without rights, anything can happen. If conservatives think President Obama's governing by executive fiat was scary and liberals think Donald Trump's executive orders were crazy, then the only answer is to reset the rules so that we don't have future presidents who violate them. We can't go back in time to change the damage that has been done, but we can plan for our future. And that starts now.

In America, everyone has the right to speak and assemble. The rules must state that we are going to not only guarantee those rights but that we are going to stop infringing them. By doing so, we allow people to be free. And then, we can be ready to have an honest debate as a people so everyone can feel engaged and be a part of this movement.

The ground rules based on individual liberty principles were promised in the founding of this country.

So far, they haven't led us astray and they won't as we go forward as a society, as long as we recommit to them.

In 1775, Patrick Henry famously ended his speech addressing the Second Virginia Convention at St. John Church, with the famous words, "Give me liberty of give me death." Thomas Marshall, father of the future Chief Justice John Marshall, said the speech was, "one of the boldest, vehement, and animated pieces of eloquence that had ever been delivered." His resolution was to organize the militia of Virginia for the Revolutionary War and to get the colony involved in the war. His words ring as true today as they ever have.

Why?

Do you want liberty or will you settle for being controlled?

How will the end justify the means?

A person who believes in the liberty interest will never believe that the end justifies the means. It isn't possible.

Someone who believes they can get a better result by controlling people will always believe the end absolutely justifies the means and will seek ways to justify whatever decisions to get there.

Throwing people in jail for gathering, not wearing face masks, being in groups, going to church—shame on us. Not because we shouldn't encourage behavior that discourages viral spread, but because we're Americans and an individual can do what an individual wants to do as long *as it doesn't hurt others.*

Giving us back those rights might feel good, but no one had the power to take them away from us in the first place. We want to believe our government has our best interest at heart. And we certainly don't want to think they're out to get us.

If you really believe in liberty, you have to be open to change. It's foundational to how this country was built.

We've been given this amazing toolkit by people such as George Washington, Alexander Hamilton, Thomas Jefferson, and James Madison. Wouldn't it be something if those Founders helped save our country again by realizing the full culmination of the vision they had?

There's a difference between what we *think* and what we *believe* are societal norms and standards. How does that change when we are in crisis?

When the pandemic hit, we were operating under the worst doomsday scenario. We thought we might actually watch our family and friends succumb to the ravages of COVID-19—or that we might die ourselves. It was so bad that we needed to shut down the American economy and, in large part, the global economy too. A lot of information was coming at us fast and furious. Some of it was real, and some of it was noise. It got to a point where it was confusing for most people.

The way the United States reacted to COVID-19 is one of the scariest things I have ever witnessed. That is not to say that the policies of social distancing, closing schools, telework, and stimulus packages to help people ger direct access to cash were wrong. They made total sense. Sometimes you have to tell people what to do. It's a valid perspective, but it isn't an American one. Outside of harming others, the words in the Bill of Rights are quite clear.

This is the United States of America. We were decidedly created different because we knew that we, as people, could rule ourselves. We didn't need a king.

Giving blind loyalty to anyone, any ideation, any leader or strategy without question is un-American. We are different because the people of this country come together and we solve complex problems together. We learn from our experiences and we build upon our history. We are a young country, adolescent in nature, but look at what this great country has accomplished in the world and on the world stage and from a world history perspective. We owe it to ourselves as Americans to understand that the only thing that has ever brought America through times of crisis has been the unification of her people.

If we are going to put our heads in the sand and pretend this isn't happening in America, then we deserve what we get: iPhone tracking, registries, health certification. How long do you think you've got before the government quiets your voice? This government is out of control.

Let us not turn the United States of America into Soviet Russia. Let us not forget the promise of the Declaration of Independence, the American Constitution, the Bill of Rights, and the Fourteenth Amendment, which guarantees due process and the American people's ability to be and remain free.

It is simply that freedom is under assault.

14

ANYTHING IS POSSIBLE, NOTHING IS GUARANTEED

I HAVE VIVID MEMORIES OF MY CHILDHOOD, ESPECIALLY TIME SPENT with my dad, who influenced me from a very early age. One distinct moment that largely shaped my outlook on the world occurred when I was seven years old. We lived in an apartment about five minutes away from my grandmother's house, and every morning at 5:00 a.m., my dad would drive me there to get ready for school and catch the bus. His job required him to get in early, so I had to drag myself out of bed and get ready at an ungodly hour.

I hated getting up that early. I hated the cold. But I valued that time with my dad. More important, it really did build character. One particularly freezing day, my dad's old Ford truck slid on a patch of ice and we went spinning.

I watched my dad control the truck in incredibly dangerous conditions. He didn't blink, and he didn't fail. He breathed in and out deeply and told me very calmly one important message that would become a critical core value for me: "Mike, you need to realize something right now. Life is hard. If you go around planning for the best result, you will be eternally disappointed. If you approach life as if there are unlimited possibilities but no guarantees, you'll work harder to make it. Perspective—it's the only way you win in life."

My father was wiser than I gave him credit for back then, but watching him manage a crisis and control the outcome in that moment helped me realize that by expecting nothing but fighting for everything, one can truly make it.

It's a core principle desperately needed to save our homeland in these difficult times.

According to legend, outside Independence Hall at the end of the Constitutional Convention, Mrs. Elizabeth Willing Powel asked Benjamin Franklin, "Well, Doctor, what have we got, a republic or a monarchy?" With no hesitation, Franklin responded, "A republic, if you can keep it."

In fact, we haven't kept the republic. Worse, we've lost it and aren't really even talking about getting it back. We are too busy responding to crises. Over the years, this famous quote has occasionally been misstated that Franklin said democracy instead of republic. The difference between a democracy and a republic is not just semantics, but is vital to our existence as a nation. "Republic" means "the public thing(s)," or more simply "the laws." "Democracy" means "the people to rule." What's the difference? Democracy is established in a majority rule, while republic is rooted in the law.

At the end of the day, when you live in a country with 14 to 17 percent of the population never being introduced to the concept of liberty interest, there is no liberty and justice for all.

In an effort to continue to control people, especially in response to the coronavirus, everyone's liberty interests have been abridged. Our government is hard at work trying to convince free white people who are used to being free that those abdications of their liberty interests are incredibly important to protect them from … black people. It's an us versus them between every Republican and every BLM person, encouraged to fight with one another.

Both sides play right into it and guess who is pulling the strings? The police state, because they don't care about who they hurt in their quest for total domination. All they want is power and control. Fourteen to 17 percent of the population going from involuntary servitude to full participation means a significant threat to the elitist structure of power and control. So naturally, they're going to reject any such notion because they don't want to share that pie.

What exactly did Benjamin Franklin mean when he said, "A republic, if you can keep it?"

Did he give us any clues on how to keep it? Yes, he did.

Did Alexander Hamilton? Yes, he did.

Did Thomas Jefferson? Yes, he did too.

We need to look backward to look forward. These were not infallible men. They were incredibly flawed men who, at the time, crafted these liberties without concern for the plight of people who didn't look like them. But that doesn't mean that their promise to us isn't one that, when applied to all, reaches its true potential. Perhaps it is time we take back our Republic and give all Americans the opportunity afforded when the basic principles of the Bill of Rights are treated as sacred. As for our nation being founded by flawed men, we are all incredibly flawed as well. Who among us is perfect? No one. That's what makes us great, interesting, and full of our ultimate potential.

What common thing do you say or do today that may tomorrow be considered evil? It was once perfectly acceptable to segregate public facilities or to prosecute sexual minorities. Humans evolve. At least we are supposed to.

How do I know this? God made us that way. The teachings of Jesus are all about evolution through service. Jesus told us we could do the same things he did and more. If that's not humanity progressing, then I don't know what is.

Evolving means learning to work together—being the hands and feet of God on Earth, to change the world. It's experiencing God through service to others. It is the most amazing way to live your life. It isn't always easy, but it is always fulfilling. We must recognize that we are not yet truly evolved. We do not understand God or our place in the universe. We fight instead of working together. We tear things down rather than build them up. Eventually our generation will be convicted for sins we can't imagine now but will certainly regret in the future. That's part of evolving, getting better. We can condemn America for her sins, our sins, but then all we destroy is the promise of something that hasn't yet reached its true potential. It would be like killing your disobedient child rather than helping them learn to behave. Our nation has a history (and present) of racial miscarriages of justice, that's true. We are all talking about it, and, these days, more and more people are realizing it. That is a very good thing. Mercy and grace are incredibly important elements of moving our society forward. And we must move our country forward to secure it for the future generations to come.

A friend of mine shared a story in which her eleven-year-old daughter woke up one morning in the spring of 2020 and said, "I'm embarrassed to be an American."

Hearing a child say this is heartbreaking.

What have we done to the America they deserve? No American should feel this way.

And then I thought about what she said. I don't believe she is embarrassed to be an American so much as she is embarrassed of her government.

You see, the government doesn't want you to think bad of *the government*. They'd rather have you be ashamed of being an American. This way of thinking for far too long has woken up a monster.

This is not free America.

We are ashamed of our government and the elites who have brought us here. Judge those in power by their actions, not just by what they say. We must take our republic back before we lose it forever. It's time to fight like our lives depend on it.

We have to find things that unite us, not divide us. It can be a new type of leader, although perhaps we've learned our lesson on that. I don't think we need one man or woman to stand up and say things that inspire us. We had that with President Obama and a certain part of the country had that with President Trump. They didn't solve our problems.

With John F. Kennedy, we had a president who not only inspired, but who was a visionary who got things done, like sending astronauts to the moon. He understood that you had to point people toward something bigger than ourselves or we would self-destruct. And we almost did. That visionary leadership is what brought us out of that. While Kennedy was a very flawed man, he used his strengths to change the course of our history in a positive way.

We no longer have that type of visionary in politics—someone capable of looking forward and not backward. We need something, someone who is guiding us to greatness, whether its curing disease or advancing space travel. We need radical dreamers in all aspects of life and society to move us forward and unite us around something we can look forward to. Simply put, we need not expect perfection from our political leaders. We should abandon this exercise, as it will never work. The pursuit of perfection is an endless chase. Instead, we need leaders who would die to defend the Bill of Rights for all Americans.

Elon Musk is someone I greatly admire for his extreme imaginative culture that inspires visionary leadership for the next stage in human evolution. His company, Space Exploration Technologies, was founded with the goal of reducing space transportation costs to enable the colonization of Mars. During the pandemic, the launch of SpaceX brought us all together as a nation, if only for a moment. Who wasn't rooting for the astronauts of SpaceX and for Elon Musk to succeed in opening a new spaceflight era? I haven't felt that excited about space travel since I was a young boy. And for those couple of hours leading up to liftoff, we stood united as a nation in an otherwise very divided time.

If we can find a way to veer from traditional political leadership and look toward a more unified and visionary way of running our country, nothing would be impossible. It would require a new way of thinking about old problems, rooted in the very strength of the foundation on which this country was born.

When we face existential crisis with a clear path toward something better, something bigger, we are united in that pursuit. When we spin around like a rudderless ship, there is less hope of something better coming out of it. When we don't have something we're focused on, everything is negative, partisan, and mean.

It is incredibly important, especially in times like these, to remember to always listen. Listen to the person you disagree with, so that you can learn about different perspectives.

When you truly listen to people, you can actually reach them.

I do not have to agree with someone to stand with them in a struggle to protect constitutional liberty. I'm proud to stand with anyone who respects the Constitution and is willing to dedicate their lives to the principles in that document. These are brave women and men who stand ready to serve the people of the United States and who are willing to sacrifice to affect great change. If I wait around for a team of like-minded people to help change the world, let's face it, the world will never change.

Freedom represents a chance of living, of having more than you have, of experiencing more than you've experienced, of reaching new heights. It is a promise of an opportunity and a construct we all yearn for. Taking away freedom is an absolute promise of a result. Which do you want? We will never get there if we don't recognize that we have to consistently be at liberty and that we have to be willing and able to defend those liberties. At an ultimate level, Americans must be ready to defend their liberty at all cost.

The Constitution provides us that right in the Second Amendment. The Second Amendment is often misunderstood, especially by my fellow progressives. But the strongest argument for the Second Amendment, the one it was written for, was that it empowered the people of this great country to take the power back from their government if they needed to do so. That right is second after speech and assembly because it is that important.

None of the other rights matter if the First and Second aren't affirmed.

We haven't affirmed them as a nation for a long time, and that's why none of them really matter anymore.

If you're reading this and America hasn't yet fallen, please know that it isn't too late. We all must do something. That's one of the reasons why I decided to fund a national civil rights law firm.

The lawsuits Nexus Derechos Humanos represents are critical to holding our elected leaders accountable. Not just the president, but also our local and state leaders. There's a difference between being involved in the legislative process and then holding lawmakers accountable. Being involved in the legislative process begins with your state government. Do you think about what state laws have negatively impacted you and which laws should change? Probably not, unless you're an attorney or accused of committing a crime. But if you really think about it, the actions of your state and local government have a far more dramatic effect on your life than the actions of your president or your congressperson.

The elected lawmaker you voted for (or didn't) has a responsibility to listen to you. Their initiatives have to come from us first. Then they can add on their own agenda. Legislators bank expected votes with legislation they carry. If you get hundreds of people to sign a petition and you bring it to your state legislator, he

Together we can keep our republic. It's not too late.

But if we remain divided, then we've already lost.

The fall of an empire is slow, until all of the sudden it can't be stopped. Not unlike matter being strung around a black hole before disappearing forever, an empire in crisis that is falling can produce an incredible amount of pain and suffering.

We stand today on the eve of America's last dawn. We can live to see another sunrise, but only as a free people. The only thing that makes Americans exceptional is our freedom. If you take that away, we're nothing special. Freedom, opportunity, and hard work are the fibers of America's promise. Hypocrisy, apathy, and division are the decay threatening our very survival. We know how to defeat these threats; we have done it before, and we will do it again.

One thing I know for sure: God won't give us anything we can't handle. God will also let us fail. It is 100 percent up to us. We unite over apathy or we die by the sword of hypocrisy.

The choice, my dear friend, is yours and mine.

What will be your choice?

PLEDGE TO PRESERVE AMERICAN LIBERTY

I PLEDGE my life to advancing the principles of individual liberty, and I refuse to
surrender my liberty to any earthly power. I pledge my allegiance to freedom
and justice over any person or government, and I commit my life to advancing
these principles.

I PLEDGE to stand for those without a voice, so that all Americans may enjoy the same
opportunity.

I PLEDGE to support economic policies that support industrial and technological revolu-
tions, keeping America on the front lines of excellence on the world stage.

I PLEDGE to support your right to say something I disagree with,
And I reserve my right to say I disagree with you.

I PLEDGE to support policies that use government influence whenever possible to
dismantle laws and regulations that restrict the civil liberties of Americans.

I PLEDGE to support and defend the American Constitution, particularly the Bill of
Rights and the 14th Amendment, which guarantees these protections for
Americans from every state and local government as well. These rights are
critical to what it means to be American, and I pledge my life to defending
these rights for myself, my family, and my fellow Americans. These rights
are not granted by any woman or man, and therefore no person may abridge
them. I choose to live as a free person and I pledge to protect the liberty of all
Americans, in any policy or politician I support.

I PLEDGE among all things to be a good steward to the rights promised by our founders,
recognizing our significant imperfections and the opportunity for growth these
imperfections represent.

I PLEDGE to never stop reaching for the true promise of America, and I will fight for the
liberty of each and every person who calls the United States of America home.

To sign, please go to **www.notfreeamerica.com**

ACKNOWLEDGMENTS

I WANT TO THANK MY WONDERFUL PARTNER AND LOVE OF MY LIFE, Richard Moore. Rich tolerates my idealism and makes big ideas work in real life. His work has saved the lives of tens of thousands of people and he never expects a thank you. He is a true servant. I also want to thank my sons. Sam is a constant reminder to me of my responsibility to fight for liberty and opportunity in our country. Sam is incredibly bright and incredibly empathic, and his art inspired me to spend the time it took to write this book. Zach has taught me how to live, love, and forgive in some of the most horrific circumstances. He constantly reminds me that humanity is ultimately good, and that it is our quest to guide our society to that good result. My family gives me the strength to take on fights for the meek and disadvantaged across the country, and I can never repay them for the peace and motivation they bring to my life.

Thank you, Mom, Dad and my brothers Adam and Timothy. You been a constant foundation of support for me. This book simply wouldn't exist without your support. I will also forever be grateful to Sam's mother, Jackie, who sacrificed so much so that her son could explore his dreams of education and art.

I also want to thank my amazing team at Nexus. These inspiring leaders have walked with me through fire, and stood with me as I placed our company at risk to fight for people no one cared about. My team cared, and I will always honor them for their commitment to serve the meek and disadvantaged. Special thanks to Timothy Shipe, my VP of support services, for keeping me on task and making this possible. My advisory board members Erik Schneider, David See, Lisa Breeden, T-Ann Johnson, Timothy Donovan, Evan Ajin, and our board's legal director were all instrumental in supporting me as I share the lessons of our collective work. Huge thanks to each and every Nexus employee, client, and anyone who has helped us serve a generation of detained immigrants and who stand with us in our eternal quest for liberty and justice in our society.

I want to thank the remarkable Mario Williams, who leads our funded NDH civil rights law firm. Mario disagrees with me often but he is almost always spot on in his assessment. He is the only lawyer whose legal judgement I trust more than my own (for me). I also want to thank the remarkable team of attorneys we have who serve our company and our amazing clients. Jessica Sherman Stoltz has supervised firms that have provided immigration and criminal defense to our clients. Special thanks to others on my legal team, especially John McKay, Victor Kovner, and Nicole Phyllis of Davis Wright Tremaine, John Shoreman, Mary Donne Peters, and Mike Gorby of Gorby Peters in Atlanta.

I consider our clients family, and this work is inspired by their collective challenges and successes. Lastly, I especially want to mention Yeremy Asig Coc. I found this young man after he had been separated from his mother at our southern border. He was being held in a camp in Chicago where he was abused. We got him released and helped him sue the "social services" organization that was doubling as a camp for detained kids. Yeremy is an incredibly special young man. He will be a leader in our new world, his intellect and ability to connect with people is like something I've never seen. May the principles in this book guide him, and our next generation of leaders, as they fight to make our Not Free America free once more.

I really need to send a huge thanks to the team that helped make this book possible. Laura Morton, my co-author, wrote with my voice in ways I could never imagine. As a writing tag team we would accomplish so much, into the wee hours of the morning. That work wouldn't have been possible without the research and diligence of Adam Mitchell. I also want to thank Jonathan Merkh and the team at Forefront Books for believing in me and working so hard to make sure the message in this book is available to those who may need to hear it as our nation hurtles further into crisis. I need to thank my entire team including Billie Brownell, Bruce Gore, Bill Kersey, and Jennifer Gingerich.

I also want to thank my book marketing team, including Jennifer Willingham and her team at Epic PR, Heather Wilson and her team at SKDK, Roger Keys and his team at Keys Media, Jason Bass and his team at Jason Hunter Design, Russ Cote and his team at Cote Brand Marketing, and Lyndsey Maddox and Logan Schmidt and their team at Digital Third Coast. Without each and every one of you, I simply wouldn't have been able to launch the Not Free America movement.

Lastly, I want to thank the growing list of corrupt and corrupting public officials, police, prosecutors, and government agents who have fueled my work to speak truth to power and stand against corruption. While I loathe the threat these people pose to our constitutional liberty, I am eternally grateful that we can still see the monsters and, that while it is far from perfect, we still have a system that can work. We are losing it every day, but each of these monsters and the fights we have with them reminds me that the biggest and most powerful monsters will always succumb to the light. May this book shine light on the corruption of the police state in the United States of America, and may that light provide a path forward and away from the Not Free America we have become.

ENDNOTES

1   "Code of Virginia: Emergency Services and Disaster Law," Virginia Law, https://law.lis. virginia.gov/vacodepopularnames/emergency-services-and-disaster-law/.

2   *Pearson v. Callahan*, 494 F. 3d, 891, reversed, https://www.law.cornell.edu/supct/ html/07-751.ZS.html#content.

3   Matter of A-R-C-G, et al., Respondents, 26 I&N Dec. 388 (BIA 2014), https://www. justice.gov/sites/default/files/eoir/legacy/2014/08/26/3811.pdf.

4   *Paykina v. Lewin*, 9:19-cv-00061, 2019, https://www.pacermonitor.com/public/ case/26731387/Paykina__v__Lewin__et__al.

5   "Booker Applauds NJ Legislation Limiting Solitary Confinement," Cory Booker, July 11, 2019, https://www.booker.senate.gov/news/press/ booker-applauds-nj-legislation-limiting-solitary-confinement.

6   "Jails Are Waiting for Them," *The New York Times*, July 4, 1917, https://www.nytimes. com/1917/07/04/archives/topics-of-the-times.html.

7   Jonathan Swan, "Scoop: Trump Regrets Kushner Advice on Prison Reform," Axios, July 1, 2020, https://www.axios.com/trump-kushner-second-thoughts-408d5a33- 725d-442a-88e4-d6ab6742c139.html.

8   Nirvana, "All Apologies," *In Utero*, DGC Records, 1993.

9   *New York v. US Department of Justice*, 1:2018cv06471, https://law.justia.com/cases/ federal/district-courts/new-york/nysdce/1:2018cv06471/497625/114/.

10   Turner v. Charlottesville, 3:17-cv-00064-NKM-JCH, 2019, https://www.ca4.uscourts. gov/opinions/181733.P.pdf.

11   *Korematsu v. United States*, 323 U.S. 214, https://www.law.cornell.edu/supremecourt/ text/323/214.

12   *Monroe v. Pape*, 365 U.S. 167, https://www.law.cornell.edu/supremecourt/text/365/167.

13 *Harlow v. Fitzgerald*, 457 U.S. 800, 1982, https://supreme.justia.com/cases/federal/us/457/800/.

14 "Booker Announces Framework for Comprehensive Police Reform Legislation," Cory Booker, June 1, 2020, https://www.booker.senate.gov/news/press/booker-announces-framework-for-comprehensive-police-reform-legislation.

15 *Black Lives Matter v. Trump*, 1:20-cv-01469, https://www.aclu.org/legal-document/black-lives-matter-dc-v-trump.

16 *Ashcroft v. Iqbal*, 556 U.S. 662 (2009), https://supreme.justia.com/cases/federal/us/556/662/.

17 *Jacobson v. Massachusetts*, 197 U.S. 11 (1905), https://supreme.justia.com/cases/federal/us/197/11/.

18 Ibid.

19 Ibid.

20 *Engblom v. Carey*, 572 F. Supp. 44 (S.D.N.Y. 1983), https://law.justia.com/cases/federal/district-courts/FSupp/572/44/2310637/.

21 *Varner v. Roane*, 5:17-cv-00080, 2019, https://casetext.com/case/varner-v-roane-1.

22 *Bostock v. Clayton County*, 17–1618, 2020, https://www.supremecourt.gov/opinions/19pdf/17-1618__hfci.pdf.

23 "Video, Audio, Photos & Rush Transcript: Amid Ongoing COVID-19 Pandemic, Governor Cuomo Announces Seventh Region Hits Benchmark to Begin Reopening Tomorrow," Governor Andrew M. Cuomo, May 19, 2020, https://www.governor.ny.gov/news/video-audio-photos-rush-transcript-amid-ongoing-covid-19-pandemic-governor-cuomo-announces-29.